PLANT-BASED GOURMET

PLANT-BASED GOURMET

vegan cuisine

for the home chef

CHEF SUZI GERBER

Photography by **TINA PICZ-DEVOE**

Foreword by **AFTON CYRUS, AMERICA'S TEST KITCHEN**

APOLLO
PUBLISHERS

To the plant-based
trailblazers everywhere:

—

dream, liberate, explore.

This is the power of gathering: it inspires us, delightfully, to be more hopeful, more joyful, more thoughtful: in a word, more alive.

—

Alice Waters

CONTENTS

From the Saucier 73

Elements 93

Breads and Bakes 119

Brunch and Breakfast 145

Small Plates 175

Soups 207

Mains 225

Desserts 297

Cocktails and Other Beverages 339

FOREWORD

BY AFTON CYRUS, AMERICA'S TEST KITCHEN

I feel like I should make one thing clear right off the bat: I'm not vegan. I simply love cheese too much to ever be able to say goodbye. But the time I spent developing recipes for *Vegan for Everybody* at America's Test Kitchen was some of the most fascinating time I've ever spent in the kitchen. Working on vegan recipes constantly challenged me to ask *why*? Why did the traditional recipe for a dish have an egg in it? What was it doing structurally there? How else could I achieve that result? Cooking vegan food challenged me to turn centuries-old culinary traditions on their head, pushing me to dig into food science and make creative substitutions that would cause equally delicious outcomes.

But a vegan diet isn't simply about making substitutions for what you can't have; it's about reveling in what you can have. As I write this, I'm gazing out over my vegetable garden—a small slice of backyard paradise that I tend to with near-fanatic devotion from spring to fall every year. Fresh vegetables and fruit are my passion as a chef—nothing compares to that first strawberry of June or that last frost-kissed carrot pulled from the ground in October. Plants are incredible, and in many ways, mysterious. They've been quietly evolving for thousands of years, and I think we growers and chefs are just at the beginning of understanding them and unlocking their hidden potential.

I know Suzi shares this same reverence for plants: I've seen it firsthand. Her own garden is bursting with life, full of heirloom tomatoes, medicinal herbs, and edible flowers ready to be turned into a beautiful meal. In her kitchen, peeking from every cabinet, drawer, and shelf, are the spices she's collected from around the world to make every dish sing. And from the moment you walk through the door, it's clear that Suzi's greatest passion is to share those discoveries with others—a near-constant refrain of "try this, you'll love it!" will fill your afternoon, and you'll come home with armfuls of seedlings to plant and new spices to play with.

This book is simply an extension of that innate generosity and excitement. Suzi's take on vegan cuisine is a riotous celebration of flavors—new, fresh, bold, and unafraid. Where I would ask, *why?* in my recipe development, Suzi asks, *why not?* The recipes you'll find here are inventive, modern, and joyous. As my garden grows this year, I look forward to celebrating with more plant-based meals at home—no cheese required.

INTRODUCTION

BY TINA PICZ-DEVOE

Can you remember the first time you ate an avocado? Neither can I. But I remember who I ate one with: my dad. He would ask, "Want to share an avocado?" like it was this amazing delicacy that we could only enjoy on rare occasions. I recall the two of us standing in our kitchen, with its avocado-green refrigerator and stove. I'd watch him cut the thing in half, remove the pit, then plop a dollop of sour cream (sorry, vegans) into each resulting pit hole. Then we'd scoop out spoonfuls of the smooth, perfectly ripened, fatty green tastiness. The feeling and taste of those simple moments with Dad are etched in my mind forever. That sensory memory is woven into the fabric of my foodie being. My dad was the first major foodie that I knew, and my mom, a stellar cook, was the constant tributary of his great desire to explore new flavors and tastes.

Now, when I cook, when I eat, when I style and photograph food, I think of my dad and mom—all of the meals Mom made for our family; all of the times Dad dragged us to another obscure, hole-in-the-wall eatery to try a dish he'd seen on the show *Phantom Gourmet* that week; all of the fall baking undertaken together; all of the cookie cutting on Christmas mornings. When I peruse a restaurant menu, I imagine what Mom and Dad might order, what they'd like if they were there. When I teach my daughter "from my head" recipes, I tell her stories of her grandparents, and how her Lola, her Filipino grandma, would never measure an ingredient, *ever*. For me, food is memory. Some of our best memories are associated with a meal shared with someone important to us.

My dad passed away eleven years ago after five years of living with amyotrophic lateral sclerosis (ALS), so he didn't get to see the start of my food photography career over four years ago, but when I style and shoot, I think of how much he would have enjoyed watching me in this role. As his disease progressed, he lost the ability to eat, chew, and swallow for the last three years of his life, which was one of the most difficult things to watch, knowing how much he loved food. This experience has rendered me extremely grateful for the simple ability to eat and enjoy a meal each day.

I know my father would be beyond thrilled to try all the food I've brought home from hundreds of shoots to share with my family. I know he'd be proud of how I use my skills and creativity, which he always encouraged as I grew up. I know he'd be happy to know that I'm doing something I love: eating and composing eye-catching images of interesting, unique, and scrumptious food created by incredibly talented chefs, like Suzi Gerber, and I am so thankful for the opportunity she's afforded me to collaborate on this book. I hope that you enjoy creating the dishes in this book as much as I've enjoyed eating all of them!

INTRODUCTION

BY CHEF SUZI GERBER

Plant-based foods are a veritable cornucopia of colors, shapes, textures, and opportunities for creativity. Finding new ingredients, and new uses for familiar ones, can provide an endless source of inspiration that can fuel your passion for adventure, travel, and cooking. It certainly fuels mine.

I first went vegan in the early nineties. I was a young, iconoclastic kid with a desire to fight for animal rights, and not much interest in the quality of my food. Back then, Tofurky hot dogs, BOCA burgers, and soy milk were essentially the only choices. Oh, and French fries, potato chips, and all that other accidentally vegan junk. The vegan diet of my youth was the diet of many teenagers: junk food. The belief then was that tofu was bland, and that most reconstituted plants-as-meat more closely resembled canned dog food than something to serve on a prix fixe menu. Vegetables were side dishes, not main attractions, and vegan diets ended up dominated by starchy carbohydrates. When popped rice cakes and diet soda stopped trending and the health food industry began to push diets that emphasized protein and eliminated carbs, I, like many others, was told by my doctor to give up veganism if I ever hoped to lose weight, be healthy, and fit in.

In the 2000s I returned to an omnivorous diet for about ten years. During that time, I convinced myself that I was *too much of a foodie*, and that I would *miss ceviche too much*, or *never be able to eat at Chez Panisse or French Laundry* if I were to go back to veganism. Based on my previous experience as a vegan, and my ignorance, I made the choice to continue eating animal products and significantly compromised not only my ethics but also my physical health—in fact, I developed a major chronic illness throughout my twenties that went into complete remission within four weeks of my becoming vegan again. While for health reasons I should have returned to the vegan fold sooner, during my ten years as an omnivore I ate and learned about some of the most interesting and well-regarded foods in the world. I experienced foods from Michelin-starred restaurants, multigenerational restaurants in Peru, and street carts in Istanbul. These adventurous experiences greatly bolstered my cooking, and influenced my approach to flavor and composition.

When I finally returned to veganism, it was a new era. I was living in Manhattan, and I saw firsthand how much vegan food and culture had developed. I was a kid in a candy store, surrounded by some of the best, from fine dining at Blossom and Candle 79 to comfort food at B.A.D. Burger and Champs. Now, there are even more incredible vegan restaurants popping up every day, and conventional restaurants frequently offer inspired plant-based options. That is, if you live in a place like New York City.

When I left New York I thought to myself: *What am I going to do? Surely Manhattan has spoiled me for all non-major metropolitan food scenes.* I realized why people think of vegan cuisine as inconvenient, obscure, and limited in its options; as raw, bland health food derived from a love generation–inspired concept or a highly processed simulation of food, not food in its own right. These misconceptions stem from the fact that all too often, people simply aren't exposed to well-prepared, high-quality plant-based cuisine. The most common vegan options in restaurants and grocery stores are the fried Standard American Diet offerings. Most people, unfortunately, do not have regular access to vegan food presented as haute cuisine, let alone to plant-based fine dining restaurants.

Vegans, flexitarians, and everyone in between get the raw end of the deal when it comes to finding great food outside of big cities, and omnivores miss out on the wonderful tastes (and nourishment!) of plant-based cuisine. While this is changing, we can't all live in the Berlins and New York Cities of this world, and geography shouldn't affect our ability to have inspired plant-based meals and conquer new culinary challenges.

While some vegan foodies and conventional chefs who don't live in creative food metropolises may recognize the potential of plant-based cuisine, they likely need to turn to veggie food bloggers and Instagram feeds to garner ideas for recipes and inventive presentations. Most vegan cookbooks resemble the prevalent restaurant and grocery store selections and focus on dishes that won't intimidate people transitioning to veganism or the veg-curious, or they share how to make veganized standard-diet hits, or the signature dishes of vegan celebrities. There are trailblazing cookbook authors who have made it possible for restaurants to add vegan options and to offer something other than French fries for their vegan customers—but with all the creativity, science, and exploration in contemporary mainstream cuisine, it's time that plant-based food cuisine became elevated in its own right. Plant-based can be so much more than just veggie burgers, vegan mac'n'cheese, and side dishes.

There are many accomplished and creative home chefs—perhaps even vegans with omnivorous partners, parents, or friends of discriminating taste—all itching for something new. With this book, it is my hope that foodies gone vegan, or those who cook for them, frustrated that the tastes of vegan gourmet are not readily available, can eat out while staying in.

This book will cover planning and developing meals like a professional chef, employing time-saving strategies, and ingredient experimentation, with an emphasis on flavor composition and attractive presentation. It will teach you what to keep on hand, meal items to prepare ahead, and how to decorate a plate and table using ingredients that most home chefs have in their kitchens, or that are easily accessible at their local grocery store.

The keys to an efficient—and inventive—kitchen are a well-stocked pantry and using the same ingredients in many different ways. You will see a lot of ingredients repeat in these recipes, much like they do in a professional kitchen, which is as much a testament to their versatility and inspirational qualities as it is to their ease of storage and mise en place and their availability. Also prolific in this book are vegan seafoods, which are not only filled with flavors I adore and many nutritional benefits, but are also largely underutilized in restaurants, packaged foods, and cookbooks.

Mainstream media touts a plant-based diet as a modern panacea for the environment, health, social justice, and animal welfare. But while the term "plant-based" conveys an air of purity, health, and botanical benefit, it is rarely lauded as the pinnacle of haute cuisine. A completely plant-based meal is often met with hesitation by those with less adventurous palates. Let's change that, together.

As a chef, discovering the bounty of plant-based foods rekindled my passion for the kitchen, revolutionized my life, and set me on a lifelong quest for new ingredients and restaurants. I marvel at the ingenuity of the early vegan chefs and food scientists who began transforming vegan cuisine from ersatz standard American fare into a culinary category in its own right. Vegan restaurants and vegan-friendly menus increase every year, and more people are making plant-based choices each and every day. While the debate over the best plant-based burger alternative wages on, likely followed by arguments over vegan chicken and vegan tuna, I invite you to join the conversation. Get your hands dirty and delight your senses with gourmet plant-based cuisine.

INGREDIENT SOURCING
WHERE TO LOOK AND HOW TO TELL THE DIFFERENCE

....

Sourcing is no small part of gourmet cooking. While many of the items in this book can be substituted, I encourage you to try hunting down the exotic fruits, vegetables, spices, and rare heirloom varieties of vegetables because it can be fun, educational, and, of course, will more accurately create the composition described. Aside from your go-to stores, I recommend seeking out Asian grocery stores, large and small. The variety of ingredients they offer, and their prices, often make these compelling outlets for home chefs with a taste for the exotic.

FARMERS MARKETS

A trip to the farmers market seems like a no-brainer, but not all markets are created equal. Seasonal selections, regions, and the size of the market all influence which farmers show up, and what they have with them. Smaller markets have fewer farmers and farmers who may be more selective about what they grow. To make sure you get the best ingredients, it's helpful to cultivate relationships with sellers. Many independent farmers have a sense for who is growing what, and may even be willing to grow items you use or need, or help you track down seeds or the farmer who has the perfect French sorrel you crave. Supporting locally grown produce not only gives you access to better tasting

OPPOSITE: Shopping for onions in the bulk bins of a farmers market

ingredients, but also brings you into a culture of gourmet food with the people who appreciate it most.

ONLINE SOURCES

The retail prices for dry goods such as nuts and spices can be so exorbitant that you are better off buying them in bulk online. Unless you don't have enough storage space in your kitchen (and I've been there—did I mention that I lived in Manhattan?), never skimp on quantity as these goods usually last in excess of one year. Cashews, nutritional yeast, and whole-seed versions of spices like fennel seeds, cardamom pods, cumin seeds, and others are best bought this way, and can be roasted, toasted, ground, or used whole at your own pace. Extra spices can be frozen for longevity, or to store in warmer climates.

RESTAURANTS

It may seem daunting to approach your favorite restaurant for access to their excess ingredients, but a restaurant can be your best source for produce you can't find elsewhere. Restaurants' ingredient buyers have relationships with produce and other foodstuff distributors, and while this doesn't always give them the price breaks you might think it does, it does mean that they have access to a wider range of mostly consistent produce and other items than you'd find in the supermarket, and they sometimes purchase in excess of what's needed. A good restaurant has a contingency plan for using residual goods (for example, specials of the night or week, broths—see page 88—and even pickles and preserves), but most will be open to someone purchasing down their waste margin and granting them some extra buying power. Unless you're buying a case of an ingredient, expect to pay a little more for quality and access.

SEASONAL FOODS, FOR HEALTH AND FLAVOR

Seasonality is an important element of gourmet cooking. It is often an element that sets standard-fare offerings apart from fine menus, and has been largely requisite in the farm-to-table and locavore movement. Seasonally grown elements taste better, with more flavor complexity and enjoyable textures than other ingredients. Our current global, year-round agricultural practices tend to alter natural growing methods. This results in picking fruit and vegetables too early, skipping over the in-field ripening and delaying the ripening (sometimes chemically) so that the produce ships firm and store managers choose when to release it onto grocery store shelves. This is how we are able to offer produce grown thousands of miles away. By shopping for locally grown foods, you increase your support of local and sustainable farms, and decrease the amount of transit time that delicate produce is forced to endure, which reduces the environmental impact of your food choices.

We have grown accustomed to a reasonably homogenous presentation of our staple foods: round red tomatoes, long yellow bananas, unbruised peaches, waxen cucumbers. These fruits and vegetables are all tarted up for showtime and don't resemble the way they would look if they had grown from an heirloom seed at a local farm or in your own backyard. Our modern produce is largely cultivated for mass-consumer goals of sweetness, size, and shelf life. After harvest, produce is selected for curb appeal with little accounting for flavor. If the full crop were sold at the grocery store, rather than sorted, the abundance would be incredible.

Seasonality is also an important element when considering health, given that locally produced, in-season organic foods are likely to be more nutrient dense, which can be correlated to their having stronger colors and flavors, and, typically, a shorter shelf life. Balance-oriented diets, like the macrobiotic diet, specifically focus on eating foods that correspond to the season they're grown in, in the hopes that biorhythms adapt accordingly. I'm sure we have all experienced cravings for fresh produce in the summer, maybe for a crisp, raw cucumber or a fresh, ripe strawberry; at this time, these foods are not only abundant in nature, but also filled with the salts, minerals, and liquids we sweat off in hot weather.

There is some evidence, albeit anecdotal, to suggest that matching the temperature of your food to your climate has positive effects on your health, especially impacting your energy, sleep, and immune system. In some of the hottest regions, cultural food traditions mirror this belief. I once had a Turkish man in Cappadocia explain to me in great detail how drinking cold water shuts your system down, and the only time to drink cold water is during winter, to help you balance the cold outside. He also said that drinking hot tea during summer is the best way to improve digestion and balance your body's temperature, acclimatizing it to the outside temperature so you won't notice how hot it is outside. It is true, however, that hot soup makes for great comfort food on a cold day spent hibernating, that heavy, starchy winter foods can give you a boost of snow-shoveling energy before nap time, and that a cold salad and iced tea may keep you perked up and acclimated to your busy professional life in the winter months—food for thought, literally.

BELOW: A farmers market bulk bin with beets

CHEF PLANTER AND KITCHEN GARDENS

I can't stress enough the value of growing your own ingredients. Something. Anything. Gardening offers up the ability to grow more interesting varieties of foods, including ones you may not be able to find elsewhere (hello, chocolate mint!—you have *got* to try this amazing herb). It also gives you access to the freshest possible items, the ability to influence size, shape, and flavor intensity, and, sometimes, with a little creative planting, the ability to create unique flavors from proximity planting and cross-pollination. Appreciation for each leaf, seed, petal, and drop of nectar really increases when you see how much time and energy it takes just to grow a stalk of basil, or get that first crop of tomatoes to turn red.

Your garden could be housed in a window box in your kitchen, a raised bed, or some pots; no matter the size, it will immediately help you realize why plants are the star of the show. For beginners, I recommend growing thyme, basil, and mint because there are varieties of them suitable for every temperament, weather condition, and gardener. The first two require a lot of light and water, and the last is hearty and can handle a variety of conditions. The leaves, stalks, flowers, and seeds all have different uses in the kitchen; they add aroma to your environment, and please the eye and palate as fresh garnishes. You can even burn dried stalks to make your own natural incense. The smell will provide a multisensory experience, with the aroma exciting both your nose and taste buds, something more chefs are experimenting with in the dining experience.

The following herbs and plants regenerate from clippings or scraps: basil, thyme, oregano, mint, onions, garlic, leeks, lemongrass, cabbage, fennel, carrots, potatoes, and tomato plants.

TO GROW FROM CLIPPINGS

Take a nice long stalk with good top leaves, remove the lower leaves, and submerge at least half the stalk in water, with no leaves below the water line. Change the water every few days until roots pop out that are good and long—the more forks in the roots, the better. Kept in water, the clippings will produce fresh leaves and keep growing for a few weeks, and you can pick off leaves while they're in this state. Alternatively, you can plant the clippings in extremely well-hydrated soil to grow larger, permanent plants, but keep an eye on them because I find that clippings that go directly into soil have a lower chance of surviving, especially for new growers.

TO GROW FROM SCRAPS

Many plants produce green young shoots, like green onions and fennel fronds, while others continue their growth around their base plant, like lemongrass and cabbage. To encourage fresh young greens to grow from scraps, keep them alive in water and harvest the new growth for use, or plant in soil, leaving just the top new greens exposed to the sunlight, and water to encourage root development.

PREPARING YOUR PANTRY

SPICES, HERBS, AND OTHER FLAVORINGS

Spices and herbs make up the cornerstone of vegan cuisine. You can take the same three base ingredients and make a radically different-tasting and -looking dish if you change a few of the spices. The alchemy involved in layering flavors in a dish is more art than science, and one thing to keep in mind is that traditional recipes in cookbooks are considerably under-seasoned as they lack the multistep marinades, seasonings, and sauces that go into a gourmet dish. Your relationship with spices can resemble a lasting love affair where you place your trust in the same dependable combos (I'm looking at you, cumin and smoked paprika), or it can be filled with wanderlust as you craft spice blends to approximate faraway regional cuisines—a successful method for home chefs who want to revisit vacation memories without the expense and time commitment of travel.

Something to consider is the way that certain herbs and spices operate. Some herbs and spices break down in heat, while some need to be toasted to activate their volatile oils. Some do well when long-simmered and build deep flavor notes, and some are so delicate that they work best raw, as bright, fresh garnishes. You can always be sure that the fresher the herb or spice—the less time between when it was cut, dried or ground, and consumed—the fuller the flavor will be, and the more nutritional benefits you will extract from eating it.

* **FRESH HERBS:** Keep in water until you are ready to use. Add the herbs as a final touch to your dish or use them to infuse flavor in oil. Even the water the herbs were stored in is flavorful and makes a great addition to broths, sauces, or cocktails (hello, basil ice!).

* **DRIED HERBS:** You need to use twice as many dried herbs as you would fresh ones to achieve the same amount of flavor. Consider your desired end goal when choosing whether to use dried or fresh herbs—for example, a dry or low-fat dish may not get much flavor from a dried herb if the dried herb requires moisture to release its flavor.

* **DRIED AND GROUND SPICES:** These are very potent. Use half the quantity of ground spice in a recipe that calls for the whole seed.

* **CUMIN SEED, AJOWAN SEED, CELERY SEED, FENNEL SEED, CORIANDER SEED, MUSTARD SEED:** Toast these seeds lightly in a dry pan immediately before using, whether they are whole or ground. Simmer in lightly bubbling oil to allow the flavors to bloom into a great masala.

* **CINNAMON STICK, WHOLE CLOVE, BAY LEAF, STAR ANISE, CARDAMOM POD:** Soak these in some water and use the water to flavor a dish. Or decoct (extract the essence by heating or boiling) these spices into a vegetable broth; add coriander seed and black peppercorn to make a great pho. Discard the whole spices before eating the finished dish.

* **TURMERIC:** Heat activates the punchy yellow color of this spice. Turmeric pairs well with fats like coconut milk (see Golden Mylk, page 361, and Cheddar Rice Cheese, page 112) and coconut oil (see Hollandaise, page 171), and its warm flavor complements the bite of black pepper. Try fresh turmeric simmered in a slightly acidic broth or juiced.

* **GINGER:** Salt and protein activate the flavor of this aromatic ingredient, best enjoyed fresh and grated or juiced (just be aware of the flavorful starch that separates in juice form). Dissolve powdered ginger in an acidic or briny marinade or in hot water.

* **ALLIUMS:** It's okay to apply serious heat to onions, but be gentle with garlic. Give onions time to soften before you add garlic to the pan; garlic cooks faster and will burn more quickly. Besides, more time for onions in your pan will mean a better deglaze to add to sauces later.

SPICE BLENDS

The most powerful set of tools you have is in your spice cabinet, and developing a relationship with them will help you understand your palate and how it may differ from the palates of your friends and family. Below are some classic combinations to help you understand the basis of flavors you may be familiar with, craving, or looking to boost. Add ingredients proportionally or adjust the quantity according to your taste preferences, and feel free to add or omit spices. Experimenting with this will help you demystify many of the flavors in your world.

FIVE-SPICE POWDER

A mainstay of Chinese and many other Asbian dishes, five-spice powder adds complexity and heightens savory notes.

* **MIX GROUND SPICES:** anise, clove, cinnamon, red pepper, fennel seed.

* **FUN ADDITIONS:** Szechuan peppercorn, orange peel, nutmeg.

ITALIAN SPICE

This basic aromatic herb blend is excellent for garnishing breads and mixing into tomato sauces and even salad dressings.

* **MIX DRIED HERBS:** basil, oregano, marjoram, thyme, sage, rosemary.

* **FUN ADDITIONS:** garlic powder, crushed red pepper, ground fennel seed, ground celery seed.

BEEFY SPICE BLEND

This can add the heavy, savory flavor boost commonly associated with red meat. Use on everything from seitan to eggplant, and keep on hand to add complexity.

* **MIX:** coffee grounds, garlic powder, soy sauce powder, ground paprika, black pepper, onion powder, smoked salt, sage, toasted sesame seeds, ground cumin.

SMOKEHOUSE SPICE BLEND

Whether it's in sausages or pulled pork, a smoky flavor is always needed to complete any barbecue dish. This rub is as delicious on carrots as it is on jackfruit.

* **MIX:** ground smoked paprika, soy sauce powder, hickory smoke powder, blackstrap molasses powder, ground black pepper, ground cumin, ground black cardamom.

CHICKENY SPICE BLEND

Herbs and aromatics often signal our flavor memory for chicken, which is otherwise bland and usually more associated with texture.

* **MIX:** rubbed sage, thyme, marjoram, rosemary, ground nutmeg, ground white or pink pepper, celery salt.

DESSERT SPICE BLEND

Create a complex flavor that's especially good in cream-based desserts, from rice pudding to ice cream, or even sprinkled on fruit salad.

* **MIX:** green cardamom powder, dried tarragon, ground cinnamon, flaked orange peel, Himalayan salt, ground ginger.

SCRAMBLE BLEND

This blend is a satisfying color and flavor booster for a tofu egg.

* **MIX:** turmeric powder, kala namak (Indian black salt), ground black pepper, garlic powder, onion powder, crushed red pepper, dried chives, dried parsley.

HERBES DE PROVENCE

A classic blend of aromatics used in French cooking. Everyone has their own variation.

* **MIX:** crushed rosemary, ground fennel seed, summer savory, dried thyme, dried marjoram, dried basil, dried lavender, dried tarragon, crushed bay leaf, dried mint, dried chervil.

THAI SPICE

Thai spice is a staple in my pantry. Combined with full-fat canned coconut milk, bell peppers, and tofu, having this spice blend on hand means you can make a coconut curry in under fifteen minutes.

* **Mix:** ginger, cumin, dry mustard, fenugreek, paprika, turmeric powder, black pepper, coriander, lemon pepper, lime salt, crushed red pepper or cayenne, garlic powder, clove, onion powder.

HARISSA

My favorite choice for heat with complexity of flavor, this dry blend should be roasted and kept whole, and ground as needed.

* **Mix:** dry roasted cumin seeds, coriander seeds, caraway seeds, dry red chilis, paprika, crushed red pepper, salt, black pepper, garlic powder.

BERBERE SPICE BLEND

This East African flavor combination has a deep, savory taste and is just one regional spice blend gem from Africa that combines roasted ground seeds and dried herbs, placing special emphasis on the seeds.

* **Mix:** smoked chili pepper, ginger, garlic, ajowan seeds, nigella, fenugreek, paprika, coriander seed, black cardamom, cinnamon, clove, black pepper, allspice berries.

GARAM MASALA

Required in most Indian cooking, this spice blend varies from family to family and region to region. Shift the ingredients as you like, to taste.

* **Mix:** cinnamon, ginger, clove, cumin, coriander, fennel, caraway, mace, green cardamom, black cardamom, black pepper.

FLOURS AND DRY INGREDIENTS

I recommend Bob's Red Mill for store-bought flour blends available everywhere. If a gluten-free option is mentioned in any of the following recipes, it can be replaced with Bob's gluten-free flour.

When converting from traditional wheat flour to gluten-free, I recommend adding ¼ teaspoon xanthan gum to every cup of flour at the same volume as the recipe.

COCONUT FLOUR

This water-loving flour holds together firmly and will form a nice crust with a sweet flavor.

ALMOND FLOUR

This flour is a go-to for bulking up a good crust, where density is desired. Substitute up to ½ cup almond flour in any recipe for added protein.

ARROWROOT

A thickening binder, earthier than tapioca. Excellent as an egg replacer in some cakes.

TAPIOCA STARCH (A.K.A. TAPIOCA FLOUR)

A wonderful binding agent, and worth using to thicken soups, stews, pies, and other soft food, or coat items and create a crispness, or instead of cornstarch.

SUGARS AND SWEETENERS

Dissolve sweeteners in warmer rather than colder liquids. Sugars and sweeteners need a small amount of salt to taste most potent.

SEEDS, NUTS, AND PLANT MILKS

Make sure to keep seeds and nuts on hand. Cashews, almonds, sunflower seeds, pumpkin seeds, chia seeds, and flaxseeds should be your pantry mainstays. Nuts can be used to make plant milk, and nuts and seeds can serve as nutritious toppings, crunchy elements, or as the basis for sauces and vegan cheeses.

PLANT MILK

You can make your own plant milk by soaking nuts for at least 4 hours, combining 1 cup soaked and drained nuts with 40 ounces of water, a pinch of salt, and the sweetener of your choice (a date, 1 teaspoon of maple syrup, or 2 teaspoons of sugar), and blending until smooth.

NUT-FREE MILK

Nut milks can easily be replaced with oat milk or hempseed milk, using the same quantity. Oat milk works well with anything acidic, like coffee (especially in latte foam), because of the starch in the oats. Hempseed milk has a superior creaminess and nutritional value when compared to oat milk, cashew milk, and almond milk.

OILS AND FATS

These are not made equal. Choosing the right fat is a critical component of cooking. Things to consider are smoke point, neutrality of taste, congealing and melting temperature, and water content (as with vegan butter).

When stovetop cooking, it is a good practice to heat your vessel, then your oil, and then add your seasoning vegetable (such as onion or celery) or your whole spice (as with masala) as the foundation for whatever you're cooking next. The pan is sufficiently heated when:

- Water instantly turns to steam on the surface.

- Oil forms a tight single ball that rolls but doesn't spread.

- A small amount of oil, like a tablespoon, melts and levels across the entire surface of the pan.

When using olive oil, never heat extra-virgin olive oil past the warm stage. The flavors diminish and it smokes quickly. Stir olive oil into warm soups, or submerge a container into hot water for warm oil on bread. It's best to use fine-quality olive oils as finishing embellishments, or on breads and salads, rather than risk deteriorating these complex flavors with fire.

EGG REPLACERS

Eggs play a specific role in cooking, and especially in conventional baking, where they are used to bind, thicken, and leaven and to add moisture, fat, richness, and flavor. When looking for an egg substitute for your baked goods, egg replacers are not one size fits all. Knowing what role eggs play in a conventional recipe will help you understand which replacer, or combination of replacers, to choose for the best results.

Types of Egg Replacers (Replaces 1 Egg Each)

- **GROUND CHIA SEEDS:** 1 tablespoon added to 3 tablespoons water. A slightly gelled texture, good for puddings and creamy applications.

- **GROUND FLAXSEEDS (FLAXSEED MEAL):** 1 tablespoon mixed with 2 or 3 tablespoons water, depending on moisture needed. My go-to for muffins, pancakes, and most cakey baked goods.

- **APPLESAUCE:** 3 tablespoons. Use when moisture is the goal and rise isn't necessary, as in a quick bread or a recipe with plenty of baking soda in it already.

- **MASHED BANANA:** ¼ cup. Use when density is the goal and not moisture or rise, as for pie fillings.

- **SILKEN TOFU:** ¼ cup. Use for creaminess and in place of custards or pie fillings.

- **BAKING SODA AND VINEGAR:** 1 teaspoon soda and 1 tablespoon vinegar. Use together when replacing the rise of eggs, as in a bread or cupcake. Works especially well in biscuits and cakes when the vinegar is delivered as vegan buttermilk (1 cup Plant Milk, page 33, with 1 teaspoon vinegar).

- **ARROWROOT POWDER:** 1 tablespoon in 3 tablespoons water. Use when binding is the goal, especially for a frying slurry.

- **STARCHES SUCH AS TAPIOCA, POTATO, OR CORN:** 1 tablespoon in 3 tablespoons water. Use for a frying slurry or when coating for an egg wash.

- **AQUAFABA:** 2 tablespoons whipped into a foam. Use to make mayo and meringue, as well as lighter cakes like angel food or sponge cakes.

BUILDING FLAVOR

· ·

Whether trying to go bold with veganized versions of classic dishes or make substitutions to avoid common allergens like soy, understanding the anatomy of flavors can help you develop complex and deep ones without having to rely on conventional heavy hitters. To broaden your knowledge base, there are a few must-try substitutions, worth learning for flavor purposes, even if you don't have an allergen.

UMAMI

This term may be bandied about with abandon lately, but it is rarely fully understood and instead is often used as an umbrella term for *savory*.

Umami is one of the six tastes—one of just five until kokumi was discovered a few years ago. (Today, the known tastes are sweet, salty, sour, bitter, umami, and kokumi.) In a nutshell, umami is the body's—specifically the tongue and brain's—reaction to glutamic acid, a controversial substance much maligned because of the artificially produced D-glutamic acid primarily associated with MSG. When activated, glutamic acid becomes glutamine, an amino acid essential to human metabolism with many health benefits (e.g. L-glutamine's ability to boost immune function, reduce inflammation, and increase energy, for a start). Foods that have high concentrations of glutamic acids are typically animal products, and glutamic acid is a key reason why meat

OPPOSITE: Spices add color and flavor to dishes, including breads like the challah being kneaded here.

is considered flavorful. Our brains receive signals from the taste buds on the tongue and mouth, and even from our sense of smell, indicating the presence of this compound—in part why many people find that they crave these tastes. That said, many natural plant sources also contain high concentrations of glutamic acid that can be harnessed for a nice umami upgrade to your dishes. Examples include:

- Toasted sesame seeds and their oil
- Toasted flaxseeds and their oil
- Cottonseeds and their oil
- Sunflower seeds
- Hempseeds
- Pumpkin seeds
- Spirulina
- Cabbage
- Broccoli
- Mushrooms

- Tomatoes
- Peas
- Asparagus
- Chives
- Tofu, and most other soy products
- Malted grains
- Gluten
- Peanut flour
- Walnuts
- Almonds

This list is helpful for subtle and bold flavor development when replacing animal products such as cheese, fish, and eggs. We positively associate smoky flavors with the proteins they're cooked in (because many of them are smoked), and as such, our smell and taste receptors connect them. This makes smoke another effective sensory trigger to use in conjunction with umami development.

KOKUMI

Kokumi is umami's long-lost cousin, and one of the tastes we associate with well-aged and fermented foods—an inextricable flavor that is complex and layered, sometimes accompanied by bold and acidic ferments and sometimes as subtle as a good olive oil.

Like umami, kokumi is positively correlated with the presence of proteins, but seems to indicate the fatty acids and calcium combined with those proteins. When umami and kokumi are combined, there is a natural assurance that complete proteins—and other minerals and nutrients that can properly break down and digest those amino acids—are present.

Kokumi flavors can be found in:

- Onions
- Beans
- Garlic
- Nutritional yeast

- Aged kimchi
- Miso
- Natto

Both umami and kokumi amplify the saltiness in food, whereas acidity and sweetness often decrease the experience of saltiness. It is important to consider this interplay when making a flavor choice for a dish.

SOY-LESS SAUCE (PAGE 77)

Soy sauce and soy amino products are heavy hitters on the palate, and their taste makes it easy to understand why these items have become central to world cuisines and vegan cooking, especially in marinades and Asian-inspired dishes. When choosing a soy-free alternative, keep the umami power of soy sauce in mind to ensure you are replacing it with a suitably strong flavor. Also be mindful of not overusing traditional soy sauce in your cooking, and think about how you can gain complexity in your flavors without it.

NUT SUBSTITUTIONS

Navigating around allergies can be challenging with vegan food, and one of the most common nut allergies that poses challenges is a cashew allergy. Cashews are central to most nut cheeses, but they are far from essential. Cashews are often chosen because their fat content makes them soft and easy to blend; however, sunflower seeds can almost always be substituted for cashews and almonds. Sunflower seed butter is an excellent replacement for almond butter or peanut butter, and sunflower seeds can be soaked and made into cheeses and cheese sauces as well. Substituting sunflower seeds for cashews by weight is a good go-to trick. You will also find rice-based cheese recipes in this book (page 112), which offer another strong and versatile nut-free vegan cheese option, and an affordable one as well.

People with severe peanut allergies might also carry a mild to moderate chia seed allergy, so when in doubt, if you are serving a person with a peanut allergy, substitute flaxseeds or hempseeds for chia seeds; if you planned to make a chia pudding, use basil seeds instead.

Blended silken tofu can often serve as a replacement for blended whole nuts, such as in Cashew Cream Cheese (page 117), and can take the place of cheese sauces and sour cream. You can swap in silken tofu for Cashew Cream Cheese in equal measurement. Nut milks can typically be replaced by oat milk or hemp milk.

GLUTEN-FREE CHEAT SHEET

For a gluten-free soy sauce alternative, consider using a gluten-free tamari, which is easy to find.

Not all oats and grains are gluten-free and some may be processed on equipment that also processes gluten, which means they can carry up to 10 percent gluten content without legally including wheat or gluten as an ingredient on the label. Gluten-free-labeled items must contain less than 20 parts per million of testable gluten, so extreme care should be taken when sourcing these ingredients if celiac disease or extreme gluten sensitivity is a concern.

When substituting non-wheat flour for regular flour in a recipe in this book, you can always use Bob's Red Mill Gluten-Free Mix. When mixing a gluten-free flour blend of your own, the rule of thumb is that you want to utilize a blend of lighter and denser flours, starch, and a binding agent.

Examples include:

- 1 cup light flour, such as quinoa flour, oat flour, sorghum flour, and millet flour

- 1 cup of denser flour such as brown rice flour, chickpea flour, almond flour, cornmeal, or coconut flour

- ¼ cup starch, such as tapioca, potato, sweet rice flour, white rice flour, or cornstarch

- 1 teaspoon xanthan gum, 1 tablespoon arrowroot powder, or ¼ cup ground flaxseeds

Different flours require different moisture levels. For example, when working with coconut flour or cornmeal, you will need to add 10 to 15 percent more liquid to your mixture than when working with almond, brown rice, or chickpea flour. When working with ground flaxseeds as a binder, you are adding substantially more dry ingredients to your mix, so you may want to reduce the amount of the heavier flour by 2 or 3 tablespoons.

PREP AHEAD

. . . .

If restaurants had staff come in at 5:30 in the evening without any prior prep and expected to have dazzling dishes plated and served by 7:00, they'd fail miserably. It just can't be done. Prep is an essential component of any kitchen, and finding a rhythm that fits with your work life and social life will not only reward you with amazing dishes that seem effortless when the time for final touches and serving comes, but also save you space and encourage you to cook more at home.

Breaking the labor into different times can make a job seem small and easy. If you're able to spend half an hour to an hour doing the grunt work the morning before your lunch or evening meal or the night before your brunch or breakfast, heating, assembling, and plating your meal will be a smooth and fast process that allows room for genuine enjoyment and creativity.

PREPARED OR CHOPPED VEGGIES

Keeping washed, ready-to-eat veggies, like sliced cucumber, peppers, celery, onion, kale, arugula, and spinach, in your fridge is the best way

OPPOSITE: Chopped celery and green pepper ready for use in a ceviche

to eat those items more often, be able to throw them into dishes as extras, or reach for them instead of the chips next time you need a snack. That said, for many home chefs, vegetable chopping is one of the more onerous, tedious, and time-consuming tasks, and having to do it is the main complaint I hear from meat-and-potato-cookers who are taking an interest in plant-forward foods. The more items you keep ready in your kitchen—from jars of different sauces to baked tofu and seitan or cut and prepped veggies and spice mixes—the more improvisation you can do and the easier it will be to focus on more elaborate techniques and compositions.

For parties or large gatherings, enlist your housemates, family, spouse, or friends as prep cooks and sous chefs. Most people can chop an onion with a little guidance, and will be happy to chop a couple things with the promise of eating an elaborate meal.

INFUSED VINEGARS AND OILS

VINEGAR

Vinegar is one of the most underused elements in contemporary cooking, outside of its use in salads and pickling, which is unfortunate because its acidity adds a nice complexity and helps to extract flavors. Its acids also break down the harsher elements and cellular walls of some foods we eat, making it possible to get a "raw cook" and causing some nutrients, like vitamin C and calcium, to become more accessible, resulting in better absorption and digestion.

Like oil, vinegar is a substrate that some herbs and spices come alive in, and thus we are able to taste them more, and even preserve them. Vinegar is also an ingenious tool in baking, as it adds oomph to your leavening, helps create articulated air bubbles, and complements sweetness, adding an openness to baked goods that prevents them from feeling thick and dense in the mouth.

Part of the beauty of vinegar is that there are so many types, each with its own flavor profile, such as white wine, red wine, rice wine, apple cider, balsamic, malt, and coconut. You can find a vinegar made from practically any fruit or sugar source. You can even add fruit to enhance its flavor and color. The best herb, spice, and fruit flavor additions for vinegar include basil, dill, garlic, raspberry, currants, calendula, whole peppers (like habanero), nasturtium flowers, lemon balm, shallots, hyssop, mint, ginger root, turmeric root, rose petals, and peaches.

I like to extract my infused vinegars in swing-top bottles. They form a nice tight seal to maintain the full potency of the vinegar, and are ideal vessels for pouring vinegar in incremental doses without the need for a spoon or measuring cup. I was taught that colored glass protects the vinegar and herbs from spoiling faster than they naturally would, but this could be an old wives' tale. In any case, recycled swing tops from artisan kombucha, beer makers like Grolsch, or even salad dressings make excellent bottles for your infused vinegars.

HERBAL VINEGARS

1. Fill your bottle slightly more than halfway with herbs or a combination of herbs, spices, and fruits.

2. Fill the bottle with vinegar, leaving about two fingers of space between the lid and the liquid line. It's preferable that your container not have a metallic lid with wax or rubber coating between the metal and the contents. If that's all you have, you need to use plastic wrap or wax paper as a barrier and make sure your vinegar doesn't touch the lid, otherwise you will end up with a herbaceous, briny, can flavor (as if it had been tainted by aluminum). Agitating the bottle by shaking isn't necessary because the acidity of the vinegar will do most of the extracting work for you, but if you want a really strong flavor in a shorter time span, a little agitation goes a long way.

3. Taste your extraction after a week to see if the desired potency is there. Remove most, if not all, of the solids if you'd like to slow down the flavor absorption when it tastes ready. Leaving some solids will mean the flavors continue to extract, just more slowly. To slow extraction down further, place the bottle in the fridge.

INFUSED OILS

Infused oils add flavor and medicinal benefit to foods. Some infusions will alter the color of your oils, allowing for interesting sauce and finishing results. I prefer infusion methods that reduce the heat in the process, which means the base oil is less affected and the longevity of the infused oil is extended. It also means that the type of oil is less important, as smoke point is less of a factor.

The best herbs and spices for oil infusing include black pepper, red pepper, white pepper, red chili, thyme, lavender, oregano, tarragon, dill, chives, cardamom pods, coriander seeds, whole or cracked nutmeg, cinnamon sticks, cumin seeds, whole cloves, sage, garlic, rosemary, and bay leaves.

Slow Cooker Extraction Method

1. Place ½ cup of the herb or herb/spice blend of your choice into the bottom of a slow cooker. If using dried herbs, they work best when fully ground; if using fresh herbs, make sure they are fully packed into the measuring cup.

2. Cover with 2 to 3 cups of oil. The oil should cover the herbs by a thick layer, so if you are using a smaller slow cooker you will need closer to 2 cups, and if you have a wider basin you will need 3 cups.

3. Set on the lowest cook setting for 1 hour, or until the oil reaches 125°F to 150°F, then set to warm for 2 to 3 hours, stirring every hour, for a total of 4 hours for optimal extraction. If making a double batch, extraction may take up to 5 hours.

Solar Extraction Method

This process takes 2 weeks, or 3 weeks if you have less sun, so summon your grandmother's patience, and gather fresh herbs, a good quart-sized mason jar, and another jar to collect the drained oil afterward.

1. Combine ¾ cup tightly packed fresh (but not wet) herbs (the best is fresh herbs washed and hung up for a day or two but not completely dry, so they're not dried

out) and 3 ¼ cups oil into a mason jar, cover with a clean dishrag or cheesecloth, and secure with a rubber band or twine to prevent flies or other particles from entering.

2. Once a day or several times a week, agitate the jar to mix, and switch which side of the jar is most exposed to sunlight.

3. After 2 to three weeks, when desired flavor has been achieved, strain thoroughly and store the infused oil in a jar with a tight-sealing lid. Store in the fridge unless using a solidifying oil (like unrefined coconut)—in which case, keep at room temperature, away from light and the heat of the oven.

FERMENTING AND PICKLING

Much like vinegars, fermented and pickled foods are under-consumed in most Western diets, and it's really a shame. We should let these wonderful flavor enhancers, palate cleansers, digestives, and preserves become the star of the show.

Fermenting helps develop beneficial bacteria, while the vinegar used in pickling is intended to kill bacteria and keep more bacteria from forming. Some vinegars help with fermentation, but most kill the bacteria that is used for fermented pickling. Cultured, raw vinegar, like raw apple cider vinegar, is a prebiotic, with enzymes that break down food while also providing food for the healthy bacteria in our digestive system. These enzymes chemically change whatever is soaked in them, and the changes fast-track the metabolic processes of cooking and digestion and open new flavors and nutrient access. Distilled white vinegar, on the other hand, creates an anaerobic environment—one that is absent of oxygen—that is not enzyme-active, making it incredible for cleaning things like wooden cutting boards, but not so exciting as an ingredient. Distilled white vinegar is the most often-used vinegar for commercially available pickles, making those pickles safe and preserved but not as delicious and nutritious as pickles can be.

Fermented foods, like sauerkraut, kimchi, and half-sour pickles, use a saltwater brine (and often many herbs and spices) to allow the healthy bacteria in our water and air to propagate, while the salt assists in preservation alongside the bacteria. The result is a crisper, more complex pickle, with a preserved probiotic, that has been fermented in a safe and controlled way: by reducing its exposure to air long enough for the good bacteria to take over.

I don't mind making a quick pickle to enhance a dish, but fermenting is my clear preference between the two—because of both its health benefits, and the way it boosts the texture, taste, and geeky fun of food and flavor development.

Basic Pickles

These recipes feature pickled cucumbers and cabbage, but this same method can be used to pickle other vegetables as well, such as carrots or beets.

Kirby Cucumber Pickles

6 or 7 Kirby cucumbers	1 teaspoon coriander seeds
2 tablespoons salt	1 teaspoon mustard seeds
1 teaspoon peppercorns	2 bay leaves
1 teaspoon caraway seeds	¼ cup fresh dill

1. Place the cucumbers in a gallon-sized lidded jar, then add the salt and 8 cups water, making sure to dissolve the salt in the water.

2. Add the peppercorns, caraway seeds, coriander seeds, mustard seeds, bay leaves, and fresh dill. Cover and shake thoroughly.

3. Place in a cool, dark area for 10 days, and then check to see if pickled to taste. Pickles should be crisp to the bite, an even color inside, and have no signs of mold.

4. Once desired pickle level is reached, keep them in the fridge up to 2 months.

Cabbage Sauerkraut

1 medium-sized head of cabbage

2 tablespoons salt

Preferred spices
(I like caraway seeds), to taste

1. Set 1 leaf of cabbage aside. Shred the rest and place in a large bowl.

2. Sprinkle the salt onto the shredded cabbage and massage the salt into the shreds, so it can penetrate every piece. After about 5 minutes, the cabbage will become soft and slightly translucent.

3. Mix in other spices as desired, and transfer the cabbage (but not any pooling liquid) to a gallon-sized crock or mason jar, packing down firmly and allowing new liquid to release and gather at the top.

4. Place the reserved leaf on top, submerging so the shredded cabbage remains below the leaf and liquid line. Use weights, such as pickle weights or another small jar filled with lentils or marbles (sealed) to help keep the cabbage below the liquid line.

5. Cover with a tea towel and rubber band and place in a cool, dark area for 10 days, then check to see if pickled to taste.

6. Once desired pickle level is reached, keep them in the fridge for up to 2 months.

MARINADES

Marinades separate bland cooking from restaurant-style cuisine. A well-developed marinade permeates vegetables and plant proteins, and is great for both centerpiece dishes and sides. A marinade is what begins the cooking process, using acids and salts to break down foods and produce certain textures and flavors.

Much like dumplings and bread, there's a popular marinade in every culture. It is often the flavor of the marinade we associate with something more than the vehicle itself, and marinating is an essential technique in the vegan kitchen. For me, a marinade is like a magic potion that consists of oil, enzymes/acid, and seasonings (like salt and spices) that with time fuse and transform into an elixir that can radically alter the state of what you put in it. A marinade can start to change your ingredients and replace some naturally occurring liquids with more richly flavored ones. Items with more surface area, or more absorbency, will adopt a marinade flavor more quickly, but items with a thick skin, like eggplant, will need to be peeled or scored to aid transformation through a marinade.

SOAKING NUTS

Although high-speed blenders, such as the Vitamix and Blendtec, eliminate the need to presoak, soaking is still the best way to acquire a smoother consistency and better all-around emulsion and flavor absorption for milky and creamy end goals.

To soak nuts, place 1 cup of nuts in a quart-sized container and cover completely with water, then cover and refrigerate overnight (8 hours). If you are in a rush, you may fill the container of nuts with hot water, cover, and leave at room temperature for 1 hour. Lemon juice and salt will also accelerate the softening of the nuts, but make sure to adjust the final recipe if it includes those ingredients.

SPROUTS

What plating toolbox would be complete without a few microgreens? Sprouts are an excellent, flavorful garnish, a fantastic way to get more nutrients and easy digestion out of grains and beans, and an ingenious strategy for adding organic color contrast to your plate.

The key to growing good sprouts—from chia to arugula—is aeration. For bean sprouting, cover seeds in a mason jar with a nylon esh and rinse and drain two times a day. A thin layer of seeds will sprout in just a couple of days, which is sufficient for a crunchy, spicy garnish. You can keep these growing in well-aerated, screened containers for up to a week. For seed sprouting for foods like chia and arugula, soak seeds in warm water for about an hour, and then sprinkle seeds in between moist towels, checking on their progress every day for a week. Keep the towels moist, and remove the top towel when greens start to emerge. You can harvest them as desired, or transfer them to soil to keep growing. If you want to harvest them to arrest their growth, a ventilated plastic bag or box in the fridge usually gives you 3 days to use them before they get mushy or spoil.

SAUCES AND CONDIMENTS

Sauces are an integral part of gourmet cooking, and can transform the same basic ingredients into radically different dishes. For example, seitan can be glazed in lemon sauce for a delicious piccata adorned with capers and onions, or it can be sautéed in red curry and served as a Thai dish. An elegant restaurant dish is normally dressed with a few different sauces, glazes, or marinades, creating complementary and complex layers of flavors throughout the composition. This quality of composed dishes sets standard restaurant fare apart from the alchemical art that a chef in pursuit of a unique combination and presentation can craft in their kitchen.

With very few exceptions, sauces and condiments should be made from scratch. Most store-bought options contain unhealthy elements, like high-fructose corn syrup, emulsifiers, coloring agents, binders, and preservatives, none of which you need and certainly none of which are gourmet. We can do better.

Sauces range in thickness, use, and presentation. Whether spooned out, painted, drenched, or dipped, sauces provide an opportunity to add aroma, heat, or color to a dish and can be served accompanying the dish or on the plate itself. Sauces can also be used to coat or cook ingredients for a bold, rich, and satisfying flavor and texture. Keeping a range of sauces premade in your fridge for later use will serve you as much as keeping a variety of pigments serves the painter. In my own home, I always keep spicy mayo, curry paste, hot sauce, Dijon mustard, savory ketchup, jalapeño jelly, and a Cashew Cream Cheese (page 117) on hand.

DEHYDRATION, SLOW COOKS, AND LONG BAKES AND ROASTS

These processes take time, but a range of plug-in countertop appliances have been designed to make it possible, and potentially safer, to set and forget these 4-, 6-, 8-, or 12-hour preparations while at work or asleep.

Dehydration is used widely in raw cooking, but is also a great way to achieve a nice dry, crisp texture for crackers, crisps, and even fruit chips or kale chips. In order to remove the water from these without cooking, burning, or removing the color too much, the items should be spread in single layers, often with airflow above and below, and heated at a low temperature (typically 70°F to 100°F), for 8 to 24 hours, depending on the food.

Most conventional ovens don't allow cooking at such low temperatures, and don't have the airflow desired. Convection ovens approximate this airflow by distributing the heat through fans, but home convection ovens also don't usually have heat settings below 120°F, although some have special dehydration settings. In any case, purpose-built dehydrators are fantastic for getting more reliable results. They're also often designed with tiered shelves to be able to dehydrate a sizeable amount at once—of course, the more you stack in, the higher the relative moisture and longer the heating time.

Slow cookers and Instant Pots are good ways to cook grains without a rice cooker, and excellent ways to supercharge a marinade, soften vegetables, and make soups and stews. Long, slow-simmered stews like borscht and sauce reductions are made painless in a slow cooker, you can also use your slow cooker to keep items warm that you wish to keep at a melted temperature.

EQUIPMENT

....

A good collection of equipment not only makes cooking tasks easier and faster, but in some cases, you will get radically different results depending on the equipment used, and different results if doing by hand. A classic example is that the amount of liquid needed increases when using a blender rather than a food processor, and the amount of time kneading dough by hand is almost four times as long compared to kneading with a dough hook on a stand mixer. The following list includes the equipment used in the book, and I recommend investing in at least most of these items to build a gourmet kitchen collection. Some recipes offer equipment substitutions when applicable, but results may vary if going outside of the recommended tools.

- Slow cooker or Instant Pot
- Cast-iron Dutch oven
- Double boiler
- Sous vide machine, sous vide sealing bags or vacuum-sealing roll and sealer
- High-speed blender
- Food processor with dough blade and S-blade

- Stand mixer with paddle, dough hook, and whisk
- Immersion blender
- Spice grinder and/or mortar and pestle
- Molcajete (stone mortar and pestle)
- Griddle, grill pan, and paella pan

OPPOSITE: Mortar and pestle sets

- 2 salt blocks (for pressing tofu, heavy cutting board or 2 weighted-down baking sheets may be used instead)
- Mixing bowls of various sizes
- Tempered glass bowls and tempered glass food-storage containers
- Knives: large (8″ to 9″) chef's knife, medium (5″ to 7″) chef's knife, paring knife, kitchen scissors (optional: a razor scissor is great for herb chiffonade, or try barber shears if available)
- Marble board or countertop
- Baking sheets, parchment paper, plastic wrap, aluminum foil
- Rolling pin, cookie cutters
- Drying rack
- Molds: silicone butter mold, cupcake pans, semi-sphere and sphere molds, springform pans, pie pans, tart pans
- Sauce bottles, squeeze and pour bottles
- Icing spatula and icing tips and bags
- Candy thermometer
- Silicone brush, tweezers, toothpicks
- Hand torch
- Whipped cream charger, smoke injector, sprayer for oil
- Spherizing kit, perforated spoon, or sphere syringe kit
- Mason jars, small jars, zip-top bags
- Tiered serving trays, serving platters, ramekins, and table props

Tools for Plating

- Tweezers, both straight and bent
- Plating forms such as a ring mold, hemisphere mold, pyramid mold, and square mold
- Differently shaped cutters, such as for cookies and fondant
- Squeeze bottle or piping bag and tip set
- Dropper
- Plating wedge
- Spice shakers and grinders
- Brushes of varying sizes and widths
- Two spoons: a slotted stainless or silicone-covered spoon, and a solid metal spoon with some weight to it
- Chopsticks
- Offset spatula and trowel
- Narrow tongs
- Spray bottles for oils or essences
- Shavers, peelers, microplanes, and spiralizers

KNIFE AND CUTTING SKILLS

KNIFE TYPES

CHEF'S KNIFE (6 TO 12 INCHES)

The chef's knife is the workhorse of the kitchen. If you only have one knife, a 6- or 7-inch chef's knife with a good slope to the front will serve you well. Make sure the handle is comfortable in your hand, that the pitch of the heel is ample to fit your fingers and knuckles, and that the bolster is shaped for a secure grip. It should have enough heft to assist in cutting denser items like beets, whole melons, or anything frozen, but it should not be so heavy that it fatigues your wrist or slows you down when doing a fine dice. Look for a straight blade if you intend to slice more and a curved blade if you intend to use the knife to chop at high speeds, using the front curve to rock the blade forward and backward—the rock and chop method.

Shopping for knives is not a time to skimp on quality. You want to have a nickel-free, high-carbon stainless-steel blade forged into one solid piece that runs from tip to end, not a blade that is assembled from multiple pieces. Keep a lookout for attachment hardware near the handle of the knife—a sign the blade may not be one solid piece—and see if you can see metal in the hilt, or the back end, of the knife; this metal is called the tang. Another thing to consider is the thickness of the tang for a sense of the quality of the original steel. The integrity of the metal is paramount. You want a knife that can be repeatedly washed and sharpened for years without getting dull or damaged, and that you can depend on to provide you with consistently good cuts.

WESTERN VERSUS SANTOKU

Santoku knives can be found in a variety of straight and curved blades, with metal, rubber, and steel grips, full tangs, attractive pinning, and elegant bolsters. They are known for possessing tiny divots in the central span of the blade, which makes cutting easier and discourages ingredients from sticking to the blade. There's a reason these have become the standard for most kitchens, professional and home.

PARING KNIFE (4 TO 5 INCHES)

The second most important knife in your arsenal is the paring knife. This knife will come in handy for intricate cuts, shaping, decorative cuts, and, of course, paring (peeling and shaving). I prefer shorter blades, and ergonomically shaped handles over straight handles, to get really dexterous knife angles. Paring knives should be used in place of peelers, which are often too clunky and indiscriminate to peel and shave accurately.

SERRATED KNIFE (FOR BREAD AND CAKE)

In the vegetarian and vegan cooking world you don't have much need for serrated blades, and it's important to remember that serrated blades aren't sharpened the same way as other knives, and may require special sharpening equipment. That makes using a serrated blade a privilege, not a right, in the kitchen. Using serrated knives for cutting anything other than meat and bread was a big no-no in my house growing up, and would incur the wrath of Grandpa Paul, a field medic during World War II and a doctor thereafter (maybe the only profession more serious about knife skills than chefs). For our purposes, serrated knives are used for cutting bread, cake, and the occasional overripe tomato; the knives with wider teeth are relegated to hearty, thick-crust artisan breads and bagels, while the blades with long, narrow teeth are dedicated to soft loaves, cake sponges, and quick breads.

CUTTING TECHNIQUES

A million chefs will have a million opinions on the proper way to hold a knife. Your style of doing this is your own, but should prevent your hand from ever curling under the knife, and should prevent diagonal cuts from accidentally creeping into your bâtonnets (page 60). I was trained to never touch the span of the blade with my index finger, unless doing fine crafting such as feathering with a paring knife. The knife hold that I teach uses a pinch with the thumb and the index knuckle on the bolster, just before the hilt. The pinch means you can use the blade as an extension of your arm and entire hand and can keep your wrist straight, without the hyper-extension of the index finger out. It's all about preventing fatigue and increasing control. With this in mind, go forth and chop.

THE CURLED CLAW

The hand that is not holding the knife—your stabilizing hand—plays an important role in the cutting process. Perfecting your ability to stabilize an item can speed up the cutting process, as the hand rotates and positions the vegetable.

The curled claw grip, used to secure the vegetable with the fingertips of your stabilizing hand, is done by curling your fingertips to create a claw, so your hand position has the space to accommodate almost any fruit or vegetable and your delicate fingertips are hidden away from the undiscriminating blade you are wielding. When using the claw method correctly, the flat span of your knuckles can serve as a guide for your blade and assist in cutting at accurate angles. Your fingers should be tucked under, making your second knuckle a vertical cliff against which to brace and guide your blade. With practice, a mutual pressure between your knuckle and your blade means your knife can follow your guiding hand across your cutting field, and then your speed and precision are synced.

BATON, BÂTONNET, AND JULIENNE
(A.K.A FRENCH FRIES): THREE SHAPES, ONE CUT

Baton, from the French bâton, meaning "stick," is a thick stick with a square on each end and long sides, and is otherwise known as pont-neuf (thick cut). Standard size is considered a square end of 1 to 2 centimeters with a length of up to 8 centimeters. A 1-centimeter baton is the beginning of the dice chop, or cube.

Bâtonnet, which is French for "little stick," is thinner, usually ½-centimeter square end and 5 centimeters long. This is how you set up the perfect small dice.

Julienne, the matchstick cut, is also known as allumette, which means "matchstick" in French. It is usually the same length as the bâtonnet, but half the thickness, ranging from ¼ to ⅓ of a centimeter. Julienne is the beginning cut for a fine dice or brunoise cut.

ROUGH CHOP VERSUS PRECISE CHOP

There are many applications where a precise chop is unnecessary; for example, when stewing or blending. That's when a rough chop is your friend. A rough chop is meant to produce pieces that are similarly sized, but not necessarily identical in shape. The cut is intended to ensure even cooking; it is used when the appearance is less important because the item will not be eaten or presented in the form in which it is chopped. Rough chops are also good for quick salads and pickling.

CHIFFONADE

A chiffonade can be used with any leafy ingredient, and results in slender ribbons that you can use for a garnish. Or, you can rotate the cutting board, or your knife position, to chop the ribbons crosswise for the chop size of your choosing. Using a dull knife to chiffonade herbs risks leaving half their flavor on your cutting board, thus removing half of the reason you cook with them in the first place. You can tell how much flavor you've lost by how much delicious green oil and residue is left on your cutting board. A sharp blade and a proper chiffonade will reduce both the time it takes to chop the herbs and the amount of oil accidentally extracted by your cutting process. For herbs and greens, there are just two steps:

1. Stack the leaves in the same direction, and then roll the entire stack into a cigar shape.

2. Slice into the cigar crosswise, knife-tip first, to create thin shreds of the herb or leaf.

TACKLING COMMON VEGETABLE-CUTTING CHALLENGES

Cutting should be basic, simple, and easy. If it isn't easy, you're overcomplicating it. With the proper approach and organization, you should be able to get more uniform cuts in less time. There are four things to consider when assessing your knife skills: speed, uniformity, intricacy, and minimizing waste. Typically, you can only achieve two or three of these feats at a time, so focus on your goal. Are you in a rush? Are you trying to dazzle with perfect presentation? Are you cooking for a large group of people? Figuring out your main intentions will help you streamline your prep and choose the right technique.

ONIONS

Please stop cutting off the root end early on. It's there to help you. You can cut it off at the end, I promise.

1. Peel the onion and then cut it in half in one rocking motion of your chef's knife, cutting through the root end such that each half-piece has half the root and stalk.

2. Position the knife horizontally, parallel to the cutting board. For a medium to large dice, place your parallel blade halfway up the height

of the onion. For a small dice, place it one-third of the way up. For a fine dice, place it one-quarter of the way up.

3.   Keeping the blade parallel to the cutting board, insert the blade 90 percent of the way into the body of the onion, then continue making sideways straight cuts all the way up the height of the onion. Remove your blade and return it to a perpendicular angle to quarter off the horizontal cuts you just made, using the same spacing you used for the parallel cuts to create mostly perfect squares. Repeat on the other half of the onion.

POTATOES

Contrary to what most people may think, a natural potato is wobbly and bumpy, and thus a difficult terrain from which to imagine extracting uniform cuts. The solution is actually very simple:

1.   If you are peeling, wash and peel first, using your peeler or paring knife to smooth out any crannies and eye buds. If you are not peeling, wash thoroughly.

2.   Squaring off your potato is the key to demystifying the cutting process. Give yourself permission to omit the irregular-shaped ends and sides of the potato, cutting them off to result in a rectangular block for full-sized potatoes like russets, or a perfect cube for smaller varieties like small red potatoes. The stray ends can be tossed into soup, broth, or a mash, or crisped and used for a topping.

3.   Once your potato is squared off, make evenly placed cuts, slicing completely through the potato, and continue until it is fully sliced, then stack the pieces on their broad side, and cut again using the same thickness as the width to form evenly sized sticks.

GARLIC

Whether using the entire bulb or an individual clove, cut the root end off, turn your blade parallel to the cutting board, and use its flat side to crack/crush the clove against the cutting board, then remove the skin. The crack is key to getting all the garlicky goodness out of your clove, and will make removing the peel much easier. If roasting or pickling, whole garlic cloves are best—in this case, you can remove the peel by rolling the garlic on a rubber surface, like a silicone cutting mat, which will remove the skin and leave the clove unscathed.

The best advice I can give for preparing garlic for use is to use a large paring knife and be patient. I know it's tedious. You can, of course, press, grate, microplane, or grind it, but my favorite technique is to rough mince on the safe side of your patience wearing off, then grab your chef's knife and break and mash it until you have a gentle mash. More often than not, I prefer a small dice or a Paysanne cut because I like the heft and kick of garlic. For creams or gentler cooking, though, a mash is preferred.

AVOCADOS

I hear over and over again that people cut themselves trying to slice avocados, and I've known a person or two to get stitches as a result. Here are two methods for safely pitting avocados:

Hold and Turn

1. Place the avocado on a cutting board and hold it so the stem faces away from you and you are looking down the long side. Hold the avocado in place with your stabilizing thumb closer to the cutting board, and guide the tip of your knife into the center of the avocado.

2. Rotate the avocado away from you while keeping the blade stable and your fingers tucked. If your avocado is ripe, the two halves will easily come apart and you may be able to knock the pit out with a spoon, or with the back side of your blade.

Remove the Pit with the Knife Blade

The first time I ever saw someone slam a knife directly into an avocado pit, I cringed, both for the fear of them cutting themself and for the brutality of dulling the blade. Nonetheless, knives can be sharpened, and this has become my preferred way to remove a stubborn pit.

1. Slice the avocado in half using the hold and turn technique.

2. Insert your knife into the pit in one quick but shallow chop, turn the knife 25 degrees counterclockwise, and pull the pit straight out.

3. Remove the pit from the blade with a rag or the edge of your cutting board.

THINGS TO KEEP IN MIND WHEN CUTTING

If uniformity is truly important to you, get a measuring, ruled cutting board as your cutting surface. Self-healing quilting boards are also a great option, and prolific bakers and chocolatiers can benefit from this level of precision.

And don't forget the chef's rule: Out of speed, minimizing waste, uniformity, and intricacy, you can have two or three, but you won't get all four. Choose wisely.

STYLING TIPS TO
MAKE A GREAT FOOD PHOTO

PHOTOGRAPHER'S NOTE

W hen it comes to styling, it's all about playing with your food as much as possible. The more fun you have with it, the more that sense of playfulness will come through in your shot. Think about color and texture contrasts. What fabric or tabletop will add surface texture without distracting too much from the main subject? How can you draw viewers into the photograph so they feel as though they are about to reach for the food and eat it themselves?

Attempt to create images that appeal to all five senses. Imagine what a steaming plate of food smells, feels, and looks like. How does it make you feel when there are sensory memories involved in your meals? Perhaps the memory of your grandmother baking when you were a child, or the comfort of mom's best, most healing soup when you don't feel well. How might color, texture, shape, smell, or the way the light hits at certain times of day affect the viewer's (or eater's) desire for the dish? When composing a shot, ask yourself, does the look of this food make me want to devour it immediately?

The plate should not always be front and center. Think of creative ways to place the main dish so that the eye is drawn around the image, not just into the middle for every shot. This gives the entire body of work a nice flow, with varied background props or soft cloth creating movement throughout the image's composition.

CHEF'S PLATING

Plating is one of the most important differences between delicious, home-cooked meals and gourmet restaurant meals. A major part of the experience of fine dining comes from presentation; it can help highlight the quality of the ingredients as well as creatively stimulate the appetite, and it can also be used as a tool to enhance flavor and the experience of discovery. To that end, sauces and garnishes play a major role in modern food preparation, serving to please the eye, compose the dish, and layer bold and intricate flavors into small plates.

Restaurant-quality plating typically uses tools that one does not ordinarily associate with the kitchen, and pays special attention to color, shape, layering, structure, balance, plate size, and shape, and often an element of sculpture or verticality. Modernist techniques can add whimsical or unusual elements that speak more to the dish's overall finished appearance than they do to the taste, but they are also an opportunity to add a surprising flavor where you least expect.

COMPOSITION

When considering composition, it's important to think of things in terms of artistic metrics like color, shape, rhythm, flow, movement, contrast, variety, and balance. Typically, compositions aim for interesting texture, which can be achieved with asymmetry, alternation of ingredients or colors, and flavor matching, where the same or similar elements are presented in different ways, such as chopped and foamed, or in a sauce and as a topping. Composition is an opportunity to engage all the senses in the dining experience, and efforts can be made to add aroma, texture, audibility, visual stimulus, and layered or unfolding flavors. The most successful compositions elicit feelings like nostalgia or curiosity, and are aimed at the diner in an interaction that goes beyond the fork from plate to mouth. Not all dishes, nor all compositions, are easy or intuitive, but they should be intentional and engaging.

The more you can come to think of your plate or dish as a painting or a design, the more likely you are to break out of seeing the elements of the dish as constrained to their function as food. Whether seeking musical rhythms, opulent color ranges, or symbolic assemblies, this is a canvas for you to express what you find exciting, and evoke the experience you hope your diners are going to remember.

COLOR BALANCE

Basic color theory names red, blue, and yellow as primary colors and orange, green, and purple as secondary colors. The complementary colors are the pairs of a primary color with the secondary color that does not include the primary in its blend, such as red and green, purple and yellow, and orange and blue. These are called complements because by combining the opposites, all the colors are present. Complementary color pairs represent high contrast, which means it is easiest to see a garnish that is green atop a soup that is red, easiest to see a garnish that is orange on top of a cake that is blue, and so on.

Another consideration when choosing colors are tints and shades. A tint has more light color present, and a shade has more dark color present. For example, eggshell blue is a lighter tint of primary blue, and midnight blue is a darker shade. Varying not only color, but tint and shade as well, allows for color combinations that increase in intensity (perhaps an ombre progression of lighter to darker greens) and striking juxtapositions (imagine sand-colored streusel on a purple blueberry pancake served with sweet marmalade).

SIZE, SHAPE, AND TEXTURE VARIETY

A great benefit of the home bistro is that you can easily offer seconds to your guests, so you don't have to overcrowd your plates. To achieve that wow factor, give each item the breathing room it needs to be appreciated. The space around an item helps amplify its visual appeal, like the white space on a gallery wall.

Unless you are going for the rhythm of uniformity, try to keep the visual texture moving with shape variety (some long elements and some squat, some curvilinear and some angular), and consider how the shape of the food and the shape of the plate interact. Abstract presentations tend to work better on square and rectangular flat plates rather than on irregularly shaped, sculptural dishes, because there is less visual competition. Excitement comes from contrast. You don't want a flat presentation, nor do you want an overly busy look that keeps the eye from focusing on key elements.

SOFT, FIRM, CRUNCHY, WET, DRY

Each one of these textures should be present in most dishes. They activate different parts of the mouth and tongue, cause different chewing patterns, and move differently over the taste buds. The longer that a composed bite spends in the mouth, the more time it has for all of its unique flavor notes and complexities to emerge. The best way to ensure a full expression of the elements is by offering a variety of compelling textures and sensations.

NOT ALL SPICE IS HEAT

Mace, clove, nutmeg, and allspice have numbing qualities, whereas basil, mint, and coconut have cooling qualities. Ginger, wasabi, and many radishes result in respiratory and outer mouth tingling, and chilis and other peppers impart an oily, central mouth heat. Salt can amplify sweetness, while vinegar can downplay sweetness. These sensations, as well as a food's serving temperature, can layer and cut through different flavors, so composing a dish to alternate bold components with cleansing components, or heating factors with cooling factors, will keep the dish exciting until the last bite.

PLATING ORDER AND KEEPING THINGS WARM

Some elements on your plate may need to cool before you assemble them, such as a frosting that will otherwise droop, chocolate that will melt, or a rice pyramid that will come apart when you remove the mold. Other elements are fun to assemble hot, such as a pat of vegan butter on your fresh biscuits. However, foods best eaten hot can often suffer at the hand of an elaborate plating scheme, cooling down before your fingers finish their composition, and losing all warmth before reaching the lips of your guests. Let's explore some tips for this:

✳ **Heat your plate.** Not only is it a sophisticated move that extends the sensory experience beyond the food itself, but it is also an excellent way to retain heat in your food, and ensures that a temperature drop won't alter the flavor of hot foods.

✳ Conversely, **chilling a serving item,** like a bowl for a hot soup, encourages extra steaming, which, while a nuisance for photos, adds to the aroma of the dish and the excitement of your guests at the table. It is also worth taking the time to chill the glasses for drinks, especially cocktails.

✳ **Warming lights** are perfect for holding composed, strong dishes while you gather all your items for service, but when overused, they can dry out a dish and create tougher textures on the top. More modern ovens may have a Keep Warm setting, which is useful for holding heat for 5 to 10 minutes, max.

✳ **A bain-marie**—a water bath used to warm items above a recently boiled pot of water removed from the flame—can provide ambient heat while you wait to plate a dish. This can also be achieved by heating a large dish of water on the bottom rack of the oven at a very low temperature, then placing the dish to be kept warm on the rack above with the heat off (for 20 minutes or less).

✳ **Making components ahead,** reheating as you go, and assembling a dish at the last minute is the method that most restaurant kitchens utilize. Some elements may be partially cooked or baked and refrigerated, or even frozen, and then combined or heated individually before assembling and serving.

FIVE CLASSIC PRESENTATIONS

TRADITIONAL

Traditional presentations typically follow the model of main, side vegetable, and starch, grouped near each other in a manner one might call tight. The composition focuses more on variety from the different dishes within the plate than on a strategic visual composition, but this is subject to interpretation. Garnishes such as crisped toppings or drizzled sauces are usually placed on top of or near the food on the dish, rather than extending outward. For a classic presentation, neat side grouping, symmetry, and central focus are paramount.

FREE FORM

The most common plating style used in restaurants today, free-form plating intersperses a few different elements for a colorful and rhythmic presentation. Items are usually alternated from one end of a plate to another. Think of baskets or tapestries, with a sort of woven and patterned effect on the plate. Long rectangular plates and zigzag linear sauces are in heavy rotation for free-form presentation.

LANDSCAPE

Landscape presentation can include elements of traditional presentation, free-form presentation, or both, but almost always includes painterly swipes or lines of sauces and beds of greens that create depth with a more forceful direction. Movement usually goes from one side to the other or around the plate, and is syncopated by other elements such as peas, droplets, or microgreens, with elements of one type usually serving as the demarcation line between different components of a dish. Think of an impressionist painting, with a hazy blue background interrupted by mountains and a green shrub in the foreground. Plate painting is typically involved, as is an emphasis on vertical lines and structures.

NARRATIVE

Narrative presentations are typically symbolic, but can also be realistic in their aim. Telling a story with the food, or having a linear or arced presentation that moves you through several tastes, may be a less common way to plate, but it is a fun way to progress through different textures or colors. Consider using a progression of leaf sizes to represent basil's growth, or making a sun wheel out of corn kernels, or floating a cream in a ramekin on a sea of blood-red borscht. Narrative presentations are opportunities for guest engagement, either intellectually or in a more hands-on way. My favorite expressions of narrative presentations are living garnishes, which guests can remove leaves from and add themselves, and multipart mezzes that guests can explore and combine in myriad ways.

DECONSTRUCTED

The most misused, and perhaps misunderstood, presentation style is a deconstructed plate. Deconstructed presentations are interesting because they expose or even highlight elements of a dish that would otherwise be hidden or combined in a way that removes their individual qualities, such as basil in a tomato soup. Taking all ingredients of a dish, treating each one with special care, and presenting them together in a different way encourages a new sensorial experience of otherwise-familiar flavors or foods—consider a baba ghanoush comprised of eggplant canapés, for example, rather than the classic spreadable puree.

FROM THE SAUCIER

OPPOSITE: Homemade pesto, preserves, and sauces

A good upbringing means not that you won't spill sauce on the tablecloth, but that you won't notice it when someone else does.

—

Anton Chekhov

Worcestershire Sauce

MAKES 1 CUP

6 tablespoons apple cider vinegar

3 tablespoons tamari or
Soy-Less Sauce (page 77)

1 ½ teaspoons brown mustard

1 teaspoon finely chopped chives

1 teaspoon ground flaxseeds

1 teaspoon cayenne powder

1 teaspoon salt

½ teaspoon onion powder

½ teaspoon garlic powder

¼ teaspoon ginger powder

Pinch allspice powder

Pinch cinnamon powder

1. Combine all ingredients with ¼ cup water and whisk vigorously.

2. Use an immersion blender lightly to emulsify, or transfer to a high-speed blender and blend until emulsified.

3. Store in a jar with a tight-fitting lid and refrigerate. Keeps for up to 6 months.

Grilled Red Pepper Sauce

MAKES APPROXIMATELY 2 CUPS

6 large red bell peppers
(about 2 pounds), quartered

1 or 2 whole cayenne peppers,
or other small hot red
peppers, to taste

1 red onion, quartered

2 garlic cloves, crushed

¼ cup extra-virgin olive oil

1 teaspoon red wine vinegar or
leftover red wine1 teaspoon
smoked paprika

Salt and pepper, to taste

1. Heat a large pot of water to a boil, add the red bell peppers, and blanch for 2 minutes, then drain and remove the skins from the peppers.

2. Heat a cast-iron grill on medium-high and grill the blanched peppers until black marks stripe their flesh and they feel tender.

3. Combine the grilled peppers with all the remaining ingredients, stirring often on medium heat, in a sauté pan and cook until they become aromatic.

4. Transfer to a blender and blend until smooth.

5. Store in a jar with a tight-fitting lid and refrigerate. Keeps for up to 2 weeks.

Scratch Cocktail Sauce

MAKES APPROXIMATELY 2 CUPS

3 tablespoons peeled and finely grated fresh horseradish	1 tablespoon safflower or avocado oil
Juice of 2 lemons (3 to 4 tablespoons)	2 tablespoons Worcestershire Sauce (page 75)
Zest of ½ lemon (a little more than 1 teaspoon)	1 teaspoon agave or liquid cane sugar (optional)
1 teaspoon white wine vinegar	1 teaspoon crushed red pepper
8 Roma tomatoes, quartered	½ teaspoon sea salt
	¼ teaspoon black pepper

1. Preheat oven to 350°F.

2. In a small mixing bowl, combine the horseradish, lemon juice, lemon zest, and white wine vinegar and set aside to soak.

3. Toss the tomato quarters in the safflower oil, and then place them in a foil pouch in a roasting pan.

4. Roast the tomatoes until they're runny and soft, approximately 20 minutes, then remove from the oven and let cool. Make sure not to roast for too long, or you risk letting too much juice escape.

5. While the tomatoes cool, combine the horseradish and its soaking liquid, the Worcestershire Sauce, agave, if using, crushed red pepper, salt, and black pepper in a food processor and blend thoroughly.

6. Taste the horseradish mixture for spice and sweetness level. If it's the desired heat, add the warm or room temperature tomatoes and pulse until sauce reaches the desired smoothness.

7. Store in a jar with a tight-fitting lid and refrigerate. Keeps for up to 2 weeks.

Soy-Less Sauce

MAKES APPROXIMATELY 2 CUPS

½ cup Basic Broth (page 88)

3 tablespoons balsamic vinegar

1 ½ tablespoons blackstrap molasses

1 tablespoon chickpea miso

1 teaspoon salt

¼ teaspoon ginger powder

¼ teaspoon garlic powder

Pinch black pepper

1. Combine all ingredients in a blender, add 3 cups water, and blend on medium speed for 30 seconds.

2. Transfer to a saucepan and boil for 5 minutes.

3. Reduce the temperature and simmer, uncovered, for 20 minutes, until the mixture has reduced to approximately 2 cups.

4. Store in a jar with a tight-fitting lid and refrigerate. Keeps for up to 3 months.

Sun Sauce

MAKES APPROXIMATELY 2 CUPS

1 cup nutritional yeast

½ cup raw or sprouted sunflower seeds, soaked and then drained

3 garlic cloves, crushed and minced

One 1-inch fresh turmeric root, minced

One 2-inch fresh ginger root, minced

1 cup Onion Broth (page 88)

¼ cup fresh lemon juice (about 2 lemons)

1 tablespoon extra-virgin olive oil

1 teaspoon Soy-Less Sauce (page 77)

1 teaspoon maple syrup

½ teaspoon black pepper

¼ teaspoon salt

¼ teaspoon yellow mustard powder

1. Combine all ingredients together in a high-speed blender and blend on high until emulsified.

2. Transfer the mixture to a small saucepan over medium heat and cook, stirring often, until mixture thickens and turns yellow from the turmeric activation.

3. Let cool, then store in a glass jar with a tight-fitting lid and refrigerate. Keeps for up to 1 month.

Red Wine Sauce

MAKES APPROXIMATELY 2 CUPS

5 tablespoons Homemade Butter (page 79)

4 large shallots, thinly sliced

3 garlic cloves, minced

1 sprig fresh rosemary

5 tablespoons balsamic vinegar

1 ½ cups red wine (a bold flavored red like rioja or cabernet is best)

1 ½ cups Basic Broth (page 88)

1. Melt 4 tablespoons of the Homemade Butter in a sauté pan over low-medium heat.

2. Add the shallots and sauté in the butter until brown, 3 to 4 minutes.

3. Add the garlic and rosemary, and sauté for 3 minutes.

4. Add the balsamic vinegar and cook, stirring occasionally, until the texture resembles a thin syrup, approximately 15 minutes.

5. Add the red wine and cook until reduced by almost half, 20 to 30 minutes.

6. Add the Basic Broth and bring to a light boil, then lower the heat and simmer, uncovered to reduce for approximately 40 minutes.

7. Remove the rosemary, and add the remaining 1 tablespoon of butter. Remove from the heat once the butter has melted. Stir to mix completely.

8. Drain to remove any solids, if necessary.

9. Use immediately while hot, or store in a jar with a tight-fitting lid and refrigerate. Keeps for up to 2 weeks.

Homemade Butter

MAKES APPROXIMATELY 2 ½ CUPS (5 STICKS)

1 cup Hempseed Milk (homemade for fat content, page 33) or full-fat canned coconut milk

1 tablespoon apple cider vinegar

1 teaspoon salt

1 ¾ cups melted refined coconut oil (the kind that is solid at room temperature)

3 tablespoons safflower oil, avocado oil, or sunflower oil

1 tablespoon sunflower lecithin powder or 1 ½ teaspoons liquid lecithin

½ teaspoon arrowroot powder

1. Combine the Hempseed Milk, apple cider vinegar, and salt and stir. Allow to curdle for 5 to 10 minutes.

2. In a blender or food processor, combine the milk mixture with the remaining ingredients and blend for 2 minutes on high.

3. Pour the mixture into a stick mold or any shape tub and freeze for at least 3 hours.

4. Keeps for up to 1 month in the fridge or up to 6 months in the freezer.

Preserves and Harvest Jam

For All Preserves

5 cups fresh fruit or vegetable puree (see variations on page 81 for suggested combinations)

2 cups sugar

Juice of 1 lemon
(1 ½ to 2 tablespoons)

Zest and pith of 1 lemon, grated (approximately 2 tablespoons)

1 tablespoon apple pectin (optional; if omitting, add the pith of 1 more lemon for thicker preserves, if desired)

1. Combine the pureed ingredients, sugar, and lemon juice in a saucepan over low heat and cook for 8 to 10 minutes, allowing the juices to fully draw out and the sugar to combine.

2. When the sugar looks dissolved and the liquid is reduced, add the lemon zest and pith. Bring to a light boil, then add the apple pectin.

3. Let the mixture bubble, stirring often, until the bubbles start to reduce in size, 8 to 10 minutes.

4. Meanwhile, boil a quart-sized mason jar (without the lid) in an adjacent soup pot, with water covering the jar completely.

5. Test the viscosity of the preserves on a cold spoon. When they have reached the desired thickness, remove the mason jar from the boiling water, transfer the hot preserves into the just-boiled jar, and use a heat-protecting glove to seal the jar.

6. Store the jar in the fridge for to 2 to 3 months.

Spring Preserves

2 cups pureed apricots (approximately 2 pints whole fresh, not dried)

1 cup pureed green apple, cored and unpeeled (approximately 1 pint whole fresh)

1 cup pureed Bartlett pear, cored and unpeeled (approximately 1 pint whole fresh)

½ cup pureed tart green grapes (approximately 1 cup whole fresh)

¼ cup chopped fresh mint

¼ cup pureed fresh fennel stalks

Summer Preserves

2 ½ cups pureed strawberries, with greens kept on (approximately 2 ½ pints whole fresh)

2 ½ cups pureed watermelon (approximately 2 ½ pints whole fresh)

1 tablespoon ginger juice or pureed peeled fresh ginger root

Jalapeño Preserves

5 cups pureed jalapeños (approximately 5 pints whole fresh)

1 tablespoon fresh lime juice

Harvest Jam

2 ½ cups pureed green tomatoes (approximately 2 ½ pints whole fresh)

1 ¼ cups pureed golden plums (approximately 1 ¼ pints whole fresh)

1 cup pureed red apple, cored and unpeeled (approximately 1 pint whole fresh)

¼ cup pureed dates (approximately ½ cup whole fresh)

1 teaspoon Madagascar vanilla extract

PRO TIP: •

Fruits can be pureed together or separately. Softer elements, like strawberry, watermelon, and apricot, may be mashed in a bowl with the sugar rather than pureed, if you prefer. If you want to incorporate harder elements, like stalks and woody herbs, a blender is necessary. Make sure, however, to avoid having hard chunks, like fennel stalks, disturbing a smooth jam.

Sour Cream

12 ounces soft silken tofu

2 tablespoons neutral oil (such as safflower or sunflower oil)

1 tablespoon apple cider vinegar

1 ½ tablespoons organic sugar

2 teaspoons fine sea salt

1 teaspoon citric acid

½ teaspoon lactic acid powder

1. Combine all ingredients in a high-speed blender and blend until smooth.

2. Store in a jar with a tight-fitting lid and refrigerate. Keeps for 2 to 4 weeks. Also works well stored in a squeeze bottle to be used for decorative finishing.

Cashew Dill Cream

1 cup raw cashews, soaked and then drained

3 tablespoons avocado oil

2 tablespoons fresh lemon juice (about 1 lemon)

2 teaspoons apple cider vinegar

2 tablespoons fresh dill, hand torn

2 teaspoons nutritional yeast

¼ teaspoon sea salt

1. Combine all ingredients and ⅓ cup filtered water in a blender and blend until thick and creamy with no lumps.

2. Store in a jar with a tight-fitting lid and refrigerate. Keeps for 1 to 2 weeks. Also works well stored in a squeeze bottle to be used for decorative finishing.

Classic Pesto

MAKES APPROXIMATELY 2 CUPS

¼ cup Basic Broth (page 88)

¼ cup pine nuts, lightly toasted

2 tablespoons nutritional yeast

1 teaspoon garlic powder

2 teaspoons fine sea salt

½ teaspoon black pepper

¼ teaspoon cumin powder

1 teaspoon lemon juice

1 tablespoon maple syrup (optional, use to sweeten if your basil is bitter)

1 cup extra-virgin olive oil

7 ounces fresh basil leaves

1 ounce fresh baby spinach

1. In a blender, combine the Basic Broth, pine nuts, nutritional yeast, garlic powder, salt, black pepper, cumin powder, lemon juice, and maple syrup, if using, and blend on low until smooth.

2. With the blender still running, slowly pour in the olive oil and blend until the mixture emulsifies.

3. Add the basil and spinach and blend until the desired consistency is reached. Take care not to overprocess.

4. Store in a jar with a tight-fitting lid and refrigerate. Pesto is best within 2 and 5 days, but keeps for up to 10 days.

PRO TIP: ·
Basil stems and flowers are tempting to use, but can leave a bitter aftertaste. Stick with bright green basil leaves, and save the flowers for garnish.

Garden Grow Pesto

MAKES APPROXIMATELY 3 CUPS

½ cup young green grapes

½ cup broccoli florets

½ cup fresh cilantro, including stems

¼ cup spinach

¼ cup fennel fronds

1 cup extra-virgin olive oil

2 tablespoons cooking wine or dry white wine

1 tablespoon maple syrup

½ teaspoon fine sea salt

¼ teaspoon black pepper

1. Combine all ingredients in a blender and blend until smooth, pausing often to scrape down the sides.

2. Store in a jar with a tight-fitting lid and refrigerate. Keeps for up to 1 week.

Regular Mayo

MAKES APPROXIMATELY 1 CUP

¼ cup aquafaba

1 teaspoon dry mustard

½ teaspoon fine salt

½ teaspoon organic sugar

¼ teaspoon cream of tartar or citric acid

Scant ¼ teaspoon kala namak (Indian black salt)

1 teaspoon white vinegar

¾ cup sunflower oil

1. In a stand mixer, beat the aquafaba for about 10 minutes on medium-high. The whisk attachment should be submerged by at least 1 inch for adequate aeration. The mixture should foam quickly, forming soft peaks.

2. Add the mustard, salt, sugar, cream of tartar, and kala namak. Continue mixing for about 5 minutes.

3. Slowly add the white vinegar and mix for 1 minute.

4. Add the sunflower oil in a slow, continuous stream, letting it drip in over the course of about 3 minutes.

5. Whip until the emulsion is smooth and creamy, and no liquids or solids are separate.

6. Store in a jar with a tight-fitting lid and refrigerate. Keeps for up to 6 months.

Mayo Variations

MAKES APPROXIMATELY 1 CUP

Spicy Red Mayo

1 teaspoon smoked paprika	1 cup Regular Mayo (page 84)
½ teaspoon cayenne pepper	

1. Add the paprika and cayenne pepper to the Regular Mayo and blend until smooth.

2. Store in a jar with a tight-fitting lid and refrigerate. Keeps for up to 6 months.

Black Mayo

5 drops black seed oil (Nigella sativa)	¼ teaspoon black pepper
2 tablespoons activated charcoal	1 cup Regular Mayo (page 84)

1. Add the black seed oil, activated charcoal, and black pepper to the Regular Mayo and blend until smooth.

2. Store in a jar with a tight-fitting lid and refrigerate. Keeps for up to 6 months.

Fishy Marinade

MAKES APPROXIMATELY ½ CUP

½ cup Basic Broth (page 88)

1 ½ teaspoons white rice vinegar

1 teaspoon flaxseed oil

1 tablespoon wakame powder

1 teaspoon dulse flakes

½ teaspoon Maldon sea salt

¼ teaspoon kala namak (Indian black salt)

1. Whisk or blend all ingredients together until well combined.

2. Store in a jar a with a tight-fitting lid and refrigerate. Keeps for up to 3 months.

Beefy Marinade

MAKES APPROXIMATELY ⅔ CUP

¼ cup very strong dark roast black coffee

¼ cup tamari or Soy-Less Sauce (page 77)

1 tablespoon red wine vinegar

1 tablespoon toasted black sesame oil

1 teaspoon blackstrap molasses

1 teaspoon Hungarian paprika

1 teaspoon onion powder

½ teaspoon salt

½ teaspoon black pepper

½ teaspoon cumin powder

½ teaspoon coriander powder

½ teaspoon garlic powder

1. Whisk or blend all ingredients together until well combined.

2. Store in a jar with a tight-fitting lid and refrigerate. Keeps for up to 3 months.

Porky Marinade

MAKES APPROXIMATELY 1 ½ CUPS

½ cup Onion Broth (page 88) with 1 teaspoon tomato paste dissolved

½ cup Onion Broth (page 88)

¼ cup tamari or Soy-Less Sauce (page 77)

2 tablespoons sesame oil

1 teaspoon apple cider vinegar

1 teaspoon maple syrup

1 tablespoon smoked paprika

½ teaspoon black pepper

½ teaspoon alderwood-smoked salt

½ teaspoon hickory smoke powder

½ teaspoon cumin powder

½ teaspoon onion powder

¼ teaspoon garlic powder

1. Whisk or blend all ingredients together until well combined.

2. Store in a jar with a tight-fitting lid and refrigerate. Keeps for up to 3 months.

BROTHS

Basic Broth

MAKES APPROXIMATELY 2 QUARTS OF BROTH

3 white or Spanish onions, roughly chopped	1 tablespoon black peppercorns
2 large carrots, roughly chopped	¼ teaspoon salt
1 bunch celery, roughly chopped	2 bay leaves
4 garlic cloves, crushed and roughly chopped	¼ teaspoon white wine or white wine vinegar

1. Combine all ingredients in a large saucepan or small soup pot. Cover with water to reach approximately 2 inches above the vegetables.

2. Bring to a boil uncovered, then reduce the heat, cover, and simmer for 45 minutes to 1 hour, stirring occasionally.

3. Drain well, pressing all the liquid out. Discard the solids.

4. Let cool and transfer to a container with a tight-fitting lid. Keeps in the fridge for up to 2 weeks or in the freezer for up to 6 months.

Onion Broth

MAKES APPROXIMATELY 2 QUARTS OF BROTH

6 white or Spanish onions, roughly chopped	¼ teaspoon salt
	2 bay leaves
6 garlic cloves, crushed and roughly chopped	¼ teaspoon white wine or white wine vinegar
1 tablespoon black peppercorns	

1. Combine all ingredients in a large saucepan or small soup pot. Cover with water to reach approximately 2 inches above the vegetables.

2. Bring to a boil uncovered, then reduce the heat, cover, and simmer for 45 minutes to 1 hour, stirring occasionally.

3. Drain well, pressing all the liquid out. Discard the solids.

4. Let cool and transfer to a container with a tight-fitting lid. Keeps in the fridge for up to 2 weeks or in the freezer for up to 6 months.

Kitchen Scrap Broth

YIELD VARIABLE

Vegetable scraps (like stems and skins) reserved from food prep

Non-brassica vegetables (such as spinach, tomatoes, and mushrooms), to taste

Herbs, to taste

Basic Broth (page 88) or Onion Broth (page 88) (optional), adjust quantity as needed

1. Roughly chop all vegetables, scraps, and herbs, then combine in a saucepan or soup pot. Cover with water or broth, if using, to reach approximately 2 inches above the vegetables.

2. Bring to a light boil, uncovered, then reduce the heat, cover, and simmer for 40 minutes. After 40 minutes, the liquid should be rich in color, all the vegetables should be very soft, and the air around them should be aromatic.

3. Drain the broth thoroughly, squeezing every last drop from the cooked vegetables. Compost the leftover solids, if possible.

4. Let cool and transfer to a container with a tight-fitting lid. Keeps in the fridge for up to 2 weeks or in the freezer for up to 6 months.

PRO TIP: •
Never add brassicas, no matter how attractive those broccoli leaves look or how much kale or cabbage you have left over. The broth will develop an unpalatable bitterness that will overpower anything you attempt to cook with it.

Pho Broth

MAKES APPROXIMATELY 2 QUARTS OF BROTH

2 white onions, roughly chopped

2 white carrots, roughly chopped

5 garlic cloves, crushed and then chopped

1 tablespoon whole coriander seeds, gently crushed

1 teaspoon salt

2 whole cloves

2 whole cinnamon sticks

4 whole star anise

3 bay leaves

2 whole black cardamom pods, gently cracked

½ teaspoon organic sugar

½ teaspoon blackstrap molasses

1 tablespoon tamari or Soy-Less Sauce (page 77)

1 teaspoon black sesame oil

1. Combine the onions, carrots, garlic, coriander, salt, cloves, cinnamon, star anise, bay leaves, cardamom pods, sugar, and blackstrap molasses in a saucepan. Cover with water to reach 1 to 2 inches above the vegetables.

2. Bring to a light boil, uncovered, then reduce the temperature and simmer covered for 45 minutes.

3. Drain the liquid, making sure to squeeze every last drop from the vegetable mix. Discard the solids.

4. Stir in the tamari and black sesame oil.

5. Let cool and transfer to a container with a tight-fitting lid. Keeps in the fridge for up to 2 weeks or in the freezer for up to 6 months.

PRO TIP: •

An Asian grocery or a farmers market are good places to look for white carrots. If you can't find them, substitute pale yellow carrots or parsnips.

ELEMENTS

OPPOSITE, CLOCKWISE FROM TOP:
Fava Bean Tapas with Ibérico-Style Mousse (page 189)
Charcuterie (page 265)
Sunchoke-Celery Root Soup (page 215)

Coming together
is a beginning.
Keeping together is
progress. Working
together is success.

—

Edward Everett Hale

ELEMENTS

Seitan Chicken

MAKES APPROXIMATELY 4 CUTLETS, 12 NUGGETS, OR 6 SAUSAGES

POULTRY SPICE BLEND

1 teaspoon rubbed sage

1 teaspoon dried thyme

1 teaspoon dried marjoram

½ teaspoon crushed
dried rosemary

¼ teaspoon nutmeg powder

¼ teaspoon ground black pepper

OTHER INGREDIENTS

2 cups vital wheat gluten flour

1 cup Basic Broth (page 88)

2 tablespoons chickpea miso

3 tablespoons tamari
or Soy-Less Sauce (page 77)

2 tablespoons sesame oil

1 teaspoon liquid smoke

1. Preheat oven to 350°F.

2. Combine all ingredients for the Poultry Spice Blend in a small bowl.

3. Mix the vital wheat gluten flour with 1 tablespoon of the Poultry Spice Blend and set aside. Transfer leftover spice into a spice jar with a tight-fitting lid and save for later use.

4. Combine the Basic Broth and chickpea miso and stir to dissolve the miso.

5. Add the tamari, sesame oil, and liquid smoke to the miso/broth mixture.

6. Mix the wet ingredients into the dry.

7. Knead for 3 minutes, let sit for 5 minutes, and then knead for 1 to 2 more minutes. Shape into cutlets, nuggets, or sausages.

8. Wrap together in foil and place the foil packet in a steamer basket. Cover, set over simmering water, and steam for 25 minutes, flipping the packet once halfway through.

9. Bake while still in the foil: 8 minutes for cutlets, 10 minutes for nuggets, or 15 minutes for sausages.

10. Use immediately, or transfer to a food storage container with a tight-fitting lid or a zip-top bag and keep for up to 2 weeks in the fridge or in the freezer for up to 6 months.

Seitan Beef

MAKES 1 LOAF, 4 STEAKS, OR 12 RIBLETS

2 cups vital wheat gluten flour

1 teaspoon cumin powder

1 teaspoon paprika

1 teaspoon coriander powder

½ teaspoon dried oregano leaves

½ teaspoon coffee grounds

1 ¼ cups Basic Broth (page 88)

¼ cup black bean aquafaba

3 tablespoons tamari or Soy-Less Sauce (page 77)

2 tablespoons sesame oil

2 tablespoons chickpea miso

1 teaspoon tomato paste

1 teaspoon liquid smoke

1. Preheat oven to 350°F.

2. Whisk the vital wheat gluten flour, cumin, paprika, coriander, oregano, and coffee grounds together in a small bowl.

3. In a separate bowl, combine the Basic Broth, aquafaba, tamari, sesame oil, chickpea miso, tomato paste, and liquid smoke, then slowly mix the wet ingredients into the dry.

4. Knead for 3 minutes, let sit for 10 minutes, and then knead for 2 to 3 more minutes. Shape into a loaf, steaks, or riblets.

5. Wrap together in foil and place the foil packet in a steamer basket. Cover, set over simmering water, and steam for 25 minutes, flipping the packet once halfway through.

6. Bake while still in the foil: 15 to 18 minutes for a loaf, 8 minutes for steaks, or 10 minutes for riblets.

7. Use immediately, or transfer to a food storage container with a tight-fitting lid or a zip-top bag and keep for up to 2 weeks in the fridge or in the freezer for up to 6 months.

PRO TIP: •
If you're looking for a vegan take on cold cuts, a thinly sliced seitan loaf works great.

Mushroom Asada

MAKES ENOUGH FOR 6 TO 8 TACOS OR 2 TACO BOWLS

6 to 8 lion's mane mushrooms

½ red onion, diced

3 garlic cloves, minced

1 teaspoon safflower oil or avocado oil, and more for sautéing

½ teaspoon chili powder

1 teaspoon chipotle powder

1 teaspoon dried oregano

½ teaspoon coriander powder

½ teaspoon cumin powder

½ teaspoon salt

½ teaspoon black pepper

1 tablespoon very strong dark roast black coffee

1 tablespoon fresh lime juice

1 teaspoon tamari or Soy-Less Sauce (page 77)

1 teaspoon blackstrap molasses

1. Using a fork, gently pull apart the lion's mane mushrooms into thick strips.

2. Toss the mushrooms with the red onion, garlic, safflower oil, and chili powder.

3. Heat a small amount of oil in a sauté pan on medium heat, add the mushroom mixture, and sauté until the mushrooms are slightly golden, but not too soft.

4. Remove the mixture from the heat and let cool. Add all the remaining ingredients and mix together in a bowl.

5. Serve hot in taco shells or combine with other elements and serve in taco bowls.

6. Refrigerate to store, and use within 1 week.

PRO TIP: •
This mushroom asada also works to top pastas or nachos, or on a charcuterie board, where it's best if slightly dried.

Jackfruit Chorizo

MAKES ENOUGH FOR 8 TACOS OR 3 TACO BOWLS

3 cups chopped fresh young green jackfruit, or two (14-ounce) cans, drained and pulled

1 red onion, diced

2 tablespoons safflower oil

5 drops liquid smoke

Salt and pepper, to taste

Sauce

2 garlic cloves, minced

1 ½ teaspoons tomato paste, or 2 sun-dried tomatoes blended with 2 tablespoons water (or more if needed) and then drained

½ teaspoon sesame chili oil

1 teaspoon smoked paprika

1 teaspoon crushed red pepper (or more, to taste)

1 teaspoon dried oregano

½ teaspoon cumin powder

½ teaspoon coriander powder

½ teaspoon salt

½ teaspoon black pepper

¼ teaspoon cinnamon powder

1. Preheat oven to 350°F.

2. Pull the jackfruit apart with a fork. It will pull apart in strands.

3. Toss the jackfruit with the red onion, safflower oil, liquid smoke, salt, and pepper.

4. Roast on a baking sheet for 15 minutes to dry out the jackfruit and bring out the flavor of the red onion.

5. Meanwhile, combine all ingredients for the sauce in a bowl. Remove the jackfruit from the oven and let cool to a manageable temperature. (Not cooled, just cool enough to handle.)

6. When the jackfruit is just cool enough to handle, add it to the bowl of sauce and mix thoroughly to combine.

7. Serve hot in taco shells or combine with other elements and serve in taco bowls.

8. Refrigerate to store and use within 1 week.

> **PRO TIP:** ·
> This jackfruit chorizo is also delicious as a topping for a salad or grain bowl.

Pickled Tomatoes

YIELD DETERMINED BY NUMBER OF TOMATOES USED

½ cup packed fresh green fennel fronds	½ teaspoon whole peppercorns
2 garlic cloves, crushed	¼ teaspoon matcha powder, any grade
1 stick cinnamon bark, broken into 3 pieces	8 red cherry tomatoes (or more, to fit jar)
2 green cardamom pods, lightly cracked	8 green cherry tomatoes (or more, to fit jar)
1 tablespoon salt	

1. In a quart-sized jar, combine all ingredients except the tomatoes.

2. Using a toothpick, puncture an entry and exit hole into each tomato, then add them to the jar.

3. Fill the jar three-quarters full with filtered water.

4. Fill a small sandwich-sized zip-top bag with water and place it on the tomatoes to weigh them down and keep them below the waterline of the jar. Seal with an airtight lid, then shake well.

5. Keep out of sunlight, at room temperature, for 7 days.

6. Refrigerate to chill before serving. Keeps for up to 6 months in the fridge.

Pickled Cucumbers

1 green pepper, cut into thick strips

4 garlic cloves, crushed

2 small red chili peppers

¼ cup fresh basil

2 small fennel fronds

¼ cup salt

1 teaspoon whole peppercorns

1 teaspoon caraway seeds

1 teaspoon dried sencha tea leaves

2 bay leaves

4 to 7 Kirby pickling cucumbers (to fit jar)

1. In a gallon-sized jar, combine all ingredients except the cucumbers.

2. Add the cucumbers one by one, moving them around to fit.

3. Fill the jar three-quarters full with filtered water.

4. Fill a small sandwich-sized zip-top bag with water and place it on the cucumbers to weigh them down and keep them below the waterline of the jar. Seal with an airtight lid, then shake well.

5. Keep out of sunlight, at room temperature, for 7 days.

6. Refrigerate to chill before serving. Keeps for up to 6 months in the fridge.

Kimchi

MAKES A GENEROUS QUART

- ¼ cup coarse salt (such as kosher salt)
- 2 pounds napa cabbage, chopped into 2-inch pieces
- 4 ounces daikon radish, bâtonnet cut
- 4 scallion greens, cut into 1-inch pieces
- 1 packed tablespoon grated garlic
- 1 packed teaspoon grated fresh ginger
- 1 teaspoon ground wakame
- ¼ cup gochujang or sriracha
- 2 tablespoons tamari or Soy-Less Sauce (page 77)

1. In a large mixing bowl, massage the salt into the cabbage until the cabbage becomes soft and wet. Cover with water.

2. Nest a slightly smaller bowl inside the large bowl and add a weight, such as cans, bags of beans, or pickling weights, to weigh the inner bowl down over the cabbage and water so that it presses down into the cabbage. Let press at room temperature for at least 45 minutes, but no more than 2 hours.

3. Transfer to a strainer and let drain for at least 15 minutes, rinsing often and thoroughly, to release the salt water from the cabbage.

4. Combine all the other ingredients in a large mason jar and mix well.

5. Add the cabbage to the mason jar and press down inside the jar until the natural liquids release. Keep pressing until the cabbage is covered with at least 1 to 2 inches of the newly released brine, then seal with a tight-fitting lid.

6. Keep out of sunlight, at room temperature, for 5 to 7 days, with a plate underneath to catch any runoff.

7. Check on the fermenting process starting at day 4. Test for desired flavor, and press the mixture to keep it below the liquid line.

8. Keeps for up to 6 months in the fridge.

Guacamole

3   ripe Hass avocados

½   red onion, finely chopped

1   stalk celery, finely chopped

¼   cup shredded fresh cilantro

3   garlic cloves, minced

1 or 2 jalapeños, to taste, finely diced

1   tablespoon finely shredded oregano

½   teaspoon salt

¼   teaspoon ground black pepper

¼   teaspoon cumin powder

Juice of 1 lime (approximately 1 ½ tablespoons)

1   lime wedge, optional, for storing

1. In a large bowl or molcajete, mash together all ingredients except the lime wedge.

2. Use immediately, or to store, transfer to an airtight container, packing the guacamole tight against the container walls to eliminate air gaps. Squeeze the lime wedge over the top, and press a layer of plastic wrap onto the surface to eliminate any air between the top of the guacamole and the container lid. This should reduce browning for up to 3 days. Keeps in the fridge for up to 5 days.

Salsa Fresca

5 or 6 Roma tomatoes, roughly chopped

½   red onion, roughly chopped

2   garlic cloves, mashed and roughly chopped

1 or 2 jalapeños, to taste, roughly chopped and stems removed

¼   bunch fresh cilantro, roughly chopped

1   tablespoon fresh oregano (or more, to taste)

Juice of ½ lime (about a scant tablespoon, or more, to taste)

¼   teaspoon salt (or more, to taste)

¼   teaspoon ground black pepper (or more, to taste)

1. Combine all ingredients in a food processor, and pulse lightly until the desired chunkiness is reached. Do not over-process.

2. Drain through a wide-mesh strainer, and reserve the liquid for Bloody Marys (page 350) or broth.

3. Taste the salsa and add additional salt, pepper, lime juice, and oregano, to taste.

4. Keeps in the fridge for up to 10 days.

Coconut Milk Yogurt

MAKES APPROXIMATELY 1 ³/₄ CUPS

| 1 | can full-fat coconut milk (approximately 13 ounces) | 1 | teaspoon probiotic powder |
| | | ½ | teaspoon agave or maple syrup |

1. Shake the can of coconut milk, then open and pour into a jar with a tight-fitting lid.

2. Crush the probiotic powder and add to the coconut milk, then add the agave.

3. Cover tightly and shake vigorously for 2 to 3 minutes.

4. Let sit in a warm area, away from sunlight, for 2 to 3 days.

5. Transfer to the refrigerator once the yogurt has reached the desired flavor and texture (keep in mind that it will thicken further when cold). Keeps in the fridge for up to 2 weeks.

PRO TIP: •
Keeping fresh coconut milk yogurt in your kitchen opens up many possibilities. You can eat it on its own or enjoy it with fruit, jam, or other sweeteners. It can also be added to many dishes for a creamy and tangy addition, especially to soups or spicy dishes like Palak Paneer (page 293).

Dulse Foam

MAKES APPROXIMATELY ½ CUP

⅓ cup white bean aquafaba

1 tablespoon flaxseed oil

2 teaspoons dulse flakes

¼ teaspoon sea salt

1. In a stand mixer with a whisk attachment, whip the aquafaba on high until it starts to foam.

2. Slowly trickle in the flaxseed oil, then add the dulse flakes and sea salt.

3. Whip with the whisk until a large volume of foam emerges that retains its shape when the mixing stops, approximately 5 to 6 minutes.

4. Use as soon as possible. It will start to droop after an hour or so.

PRO TIP: •

Foams are an excellent way to add a little modern flair to any food or dish where happy little clouds or a salty flavor pop would be welcome. I like to pair this foam with fish dishes, such as the Escargot Amuse-Bouche (page 184) and the Ahi Tuna Steak (page 257). You can use this same method to foam other flavors for different applications by swapping out the fishy dulse for smoked paprika, or even fruit powders for a sweeter result.

Smoked Salmon

1 large Roma tomato

¼ cup Basic Broth (page 88)

1 tablespoon rice vinegar

1 teaspoon apple cider vinegar

1 teaspoon wakame powder

½ teaspoon sea salt

¼ teaspoon kala namak (Indian black salt)

¼ teaspoon smoked paprika

Pinch dulse flakes

Pinch black pepper

1. Quarter the tomato for sashimi or halve the tomato for lox, and then cut lengthwise and carefully use your chef's knife to remove the skin.

2. Combine all the remaining ingredients together to make a marinade. Add the tomato and transfer to the fridge to soak in the marinade overnight.

3. Drain well before serving. Keeps for up to 1 week in the fridge.

PRO TIP: •

I like to use a garlic infused rice vinegar here (page 44), but you can also buy garlic infused rice vinegar at Asian markets.

Eggplant Sausage

2 Japanese eggplants

2 tablespoons tamari or Soy-Less Sauce (page 77)

1 teaspoon liquid smoke

1 tablespoon coffee grounds

1 ½ teaspoons smoked paprika

1 teaspoon cumin powder

½ teaspoon cracked pink peppercorns

1. Cut the ends off the eggplants, so all ends are flat. Do not remove skin.

2. Halve each eggplant by cutting crosswise, using a straight line. Score an X on the flat ends of each piece of eggplant with the knife.

3. Gently score light rings around the sides of each eggplant, spacing the rings 1 inch apart. Be careful not to make the score cuts too close together.

4. Mix all the remaining ingredients together in a bowl. Add the eggplant and marinate in the mixture for 30 minutes at room temperature.

5. Preheat oven to 375°F.

6. Remove the eggplant from the bowl, reserving the marinade. Wrap each section of marinated eggplant loosely in foil, leaving room to add 1 tablespoon of marinade to the packet.

7. Bake in foil on a baking sheet for 10 minutes, then open the foil wraps, turn the pieces of eggplant, and paint each one with more marinade. Close the foil and bake for 10 more minutes.

8. Remove the eggplant from the foil packets and bake open on the baking sheet for an additional 8 minutes, or until the pieces are mostly dry and resemble the look and texture of a smoked sausage.

9. After removing the eggplant sausages from the heat, dip the ends of each one in the reserved marinade. Let the sausages cool just enough so that they can be comfortably handled with your bare hands, and then paint again with the marinade.

10. Serve warm immediately, or wrap the sausages in foil if storing in the fridge. Keeps for up to 5 days.

PRO TIP: •
If you are on top of your make-ahead prep, Porky Marinade (page 87) may be used in addition to or instead of this recipe's marinade to give a strong, smokey supercharge.

Black Garlic

MAKES 5 OR 6 BULBS

5 or 6 intact garlic bulbs

1. Place garlic bulbs gently in a single layer on the bottom of a slow cooker. Avoid crowding. Their thin skin can touch slightly, but the contact should be minimal at most. Cover, set to warm, and let sit for 3 weeks.

2. If after 3 weeks, the paper is amber colored and the cloves are soft but not mushy, they are ready. If not, up to 6 more weeks may be required for full fermentation. Check every 2 weeks after the initial 3 weeks.

3. Store in a zip-top bag in the fridge. Keeps for up to 6 months.

PRO TIP: •
Store-bought black garlic can be hard to find and expensive. Its sweet taste is like that of a semisolid molasses. It's delicious on its own, but I also use it on a Charcuterie plate (page 265), add it to sauces or atop crostini, and even incorporate it into daring desserts. While it is simple to make, it requires a lot of patience while you wait for it to be ready. The cooking process will fill your kitchen with a garlic smell—which is great for chasing away vampires and mosquitos, but you may want to keep the slow cooker in the basement, or individually enclose the bulbs in mason jars inside the slow cooker, to reduce the odor.

Tapenade

1 eggplant, cut into large cubes

1 tablespoon safflower oil

1 teaspoon fresh rosemary

½ teaspoon dried oregano

¼ teaspoon salt

Pinch black pepper

4 ounces sun-dried tomatoes

¼ cup Halkidiki or Castelvetrano olives

1 tablespoon olive brine

¼ cup packed fresh basil

Peel of ½ lemon, shredded

2 tablespoons extra-virgin olive oil

1 ½ tablespoons crushed red pepper

½ teaspoon salt

1. Preheat oven to 400°F.

2. Toss the eggplant with the safflower oil, rosemary, oregano, salt, and black pepper, then roast for 30 minutes.

3. Combine all of the remaining ingredients with the roasted eggplant in a food processor and pulse to combine, leaving the mixture even but chunky.

4. Let cool, then transfer to a jar with a tight-fitting lid and refrigerate. Serve chilled or at room temperature. Best consumed within 1 week, but keeps for up to 2 weeks.

PRO TIP: ·

Halkidiki olives are young, large, sweet, and tangy green olives cured in brine. Castelvetranos are young, small- to medium-sized green olives with a buttery and meaty bite, and are cured briefly in lye and mostly rinsed in water, preserving the young flavor. One of the leading olive producers, Divina, offers a Halkidiki cured in the method of a Castelvetrano, known as a Frescatrano, and it is truly delightful.

Polenta from Scratch

MAKES 5 CUPS OF FORMED POLENTA OR 6 CUPS OF LOOSE WET POLENTA

3 ½ cups Basic Broth (page 88)

1 cup soy milk or pea milk (a high-fat, high-protein plant milk)

3 tablespoons Homemade Butter (page 79)

2 cups polenta corn grits (medium, not quick-cooking)

¼ cup nutritional yeast

¼ cup finely chopped fresh basil

3 tablespoons chopped fresh parsley

2 tablespoons chopped fresh oregano

1 ½ teaspoons crushed rosemary

¼ teaspoon salt

1. Bring the Basic Broth and soy milk to a boil in a saucepan, then melt in the Homemade Butter.

2. When the liquid reaches a rolling boil, whisk in the polenta. Stir vigorously, cooking until the polenta thickens and begins to shrink away from the edge of the pan, then remove from the heat and stir in all the remaining ingredients.

3. Let cool completely, transfer to the desired shape vessel (see Pro Tip), and refrigerate until set, approximately 4 hours.

4. Store in a glass food storage container in the fridge. Keeps for up to 2 weeks.

PRO TIP: •
Different molding vessels will be needed for different polenta dishes. In a dish like the Tian on page 281, for example, you should use a silicone cupcake pan to make perfect discs. For an item like Polenta Fries (page 240), you should use a shallow brownie pan or 1-inch-deep cake pan.

CHEESES

Feta

5 ounces firm tofu in block form, drained

¼ cup finely chopped parsley

2 teaspoons nutritional yeast

½ teaspoon fresh lemon juice

½ teaspoon dry and crisp white wine, like Pinot Gris or Sauvignon Blanc

1. Place the tofu block between 2 salt blocks and let press for 10 minutes.

2. Place the pressed tofu in a large mixing bowl, add all the remaining ingredients, and mash with a potato ricer. Break apart all the flat edges and mash until the desired texture is reached. Fluff with a fork.

3. Store in an airtight container in the fridge. Keeps for up to 2 weeks.

Ricotta

5 ounces firm tofu

2 teaspoons nutritional yeast

1 teaspoon salt

½ teaspoon black pepper

¼ teaspoon apple cider vinegar

1 teaspoon evaporated cane juice, dissolved in 2 tablespoons lukewarm water

¼ cup finely chopped fresh Genovese basil (optional)

1. Drain the tofu well, for about 5 minutes, but do not press.

2. Place the drained tofu in a large mixing bowl, add all the remaining ingredients, and mash with a potato ricer. Break apart all the flat edges and mash until the desired texture is reached. Fluff with a fork.

3. Store in an airtight container in the fridge. Keeps for up to 2 weeks.

Cauliflower Ricotta

MAKES APPROXIMATELY 2 ½ CUPS

½ head cauliflower, chopped (omit any greens)

3 tablespoons nutritional yeast

1 teaspoon dried basil

½ teaspoon salt

½ teaspoon black pepper

½ cup Basic Broth (page 88), or more for moist ricotta

1 teaspoon fresh lemon juice

1. Combine all ingredients in a food processor and pulse gently until the desired texture is reached, adding more Basic Broth if you prefer a ricotta with more moisture.

2. Store in an airtight container in the fridge. Keeps for up to 2 weeks.

Squash Cheese

MAKES APPROXIMATELY 1 QUART

3 Yukon Gold potatoes, cut into large cubes

1 butternut squash, peeled and cubed

1 red onion, chopped

4 large garlic cloves, quartered

Neutral cooking oil (safflower oil, sunflower oil, or avocado oil)

1 cup nutritional yeast

1 ¼ teaspoons salt

½ teaspoon black pepper

¼ teaspoon cumin powder

¼ teaspoon turmeric powder

⅛ teaspoon smoked paprika

1 cup Basic Broth (page 88)

1. Preheat oven to 400°F.

2. On a baking sheet, toss the potatoes, squash, onion, and garlic in the cooking oil and roast for 25 to 30 minutes, until soft.

3. Divide the vegetables in half, and add one half to the blender with all the remaining ingredients. Once blended down, add in the remaining vegetables and blend until smooth.

4. While this cheese is best served warm, it's also okay to serve cold: Let cool, transfer to a jar with a tight-fitting lid, and refrigerate. Keeps in the fridge for up to 2 weeks.

Rice Cheeses

Cultured Coconut Milk

1   can full-fat coconut milk (approximately 13 ounces), refrigerated overnight

1   teaspoon 20 billion CFU probiotic powder, or 2 capsules vegan-friendly 10 CFU probiotic loose powder pills, capsules removed

Bulk Base

1   cup rice, cooked in 6 cups water

⅓   cup dehydrated potato flakes

1   tablespoon apple cider vinegar

Cheese Base (Mild White Cheese)

1   cup Bulk Base (see above)

⅓   cup dehydrated potato flakes

1   tablespoon nutritional yeast

1 ½ teaspoons carrageenan

1   teaspoon salt

½   teaspoon lactic acid

½   teaspoon cream of tartar

1   tablespoon coconut oil

1   teaspoon apple cider vinegar

¼   cup Cultured Coconut Milk (see above)

Cheddar Flavor Addition

3   tablespoons nutritional yeast

2   teaspoons salt

2   teaspoons lactic acid

2   teaspoons onion powder

1   ½ teaspoons turmeric powder

1   teaspoon garlic powder

¼   teaspoon dry mustard

¼   teaspoon black pepper

2   teaspoons tomato paste

2   teaspoons apple cider vinegar

Mozzarella Flavor Addition

2   teaspoons salt

2   teaspoons lactic acid

¼   teaspoon black pepper

2   teaspoons apple cider vinegar

1. Whisk the coconut milk with the probiotic powder. Let culture in the fridge for at least 12 hours, but no more than 20 hours. Too little and your culture hasn't gotten strong enough; too much and you'll end up with an overly powerful and sour culture.

2. Combine the ingredients for the Bulk Base, or use from a previous batch.

3. Combine all ingredients for the Cheese Base, *except* for the Cultured Coconut Milk, and all ingredients of your preferred flavor addition, if using, in a saucepan over medium heat. Stir until the mixture begins to thicken.

4. Remove from the heat and stir in the Cultured Coconut Milk. Whisk thoroughly.

5. Place the mixture in a glass storage container or silicone mold and refrigerate overnight to set.

6. The cheese can be kept in the same glass storage container with a tight-fitting lid, or removed from the mold and placed in a zip-top bag once set. Keeps for up to 1 month in the fridge.

PRO TIP: •
The bulk base makes it easy to make multiple types of cheeses at once. Divide your base and make your week or month's worth of mozzarella and cheddar at the same time, or save the extra base for up to 1 week in the fridge.

Brie

2 cups Bulk Base (page 112)

¼ cup Hempseed Milk (page 33)

2 tablespoons coconut oil

½ teaspoon apple cider vinegar

1 ½ tablespoons carrageenan

1 tablespoon nutritional yeast

1 ½ teaspoons lactic acid

1 ½ teaspoons salt

½ teaspoon cream of tartar

¼ cup Cultured Coconut Milk (page 112)

1 tablespoon extra-fine activated charcoal

1 teaspoon fine sea salt

1 teaspoon powdered herbes de Provence (optional)

1. Combine the Bulk Base, Hempseed Milk, coconut oil, apple cider vinegar, carrageenan, nutritional yeast, lactic acid, salt, and cream of tartar in a saucepan over medium heat. Stir until the mixture begins to thicken.

2. Remove from the heat, stir in the Cultured Coconut Milk, and whisk thoroughly.

3. Place in a mold, such as a cupcake pan, glass food storage container, or 7-inch cake pan (well greased or lined with parchment or vegan wax paper) if making a 7-inch wheel. Refrigerate overnight to set.

4. Once set, remove the cheese from the mold and place on a piece of cheesecloth on a clean surface. Combine the activated charcoal, sea salt, and herbes de Provence, if using, and sprinkle the mixture over the cheese to coat all sides evenly.

5. Wrap the cheese in two layers of cheesecloth and then wrap with wax paper. Return to the fridge to let age for 3 to 5 days, flipping at least once a day.

6. After 3 days, check the progression of skin forming on the outside. Continue to age until the desired rind has formed.

7. After the desired rind has formed, the brie can be kept in a glass storage container with a tight-fitting lid, or can be transferred to a zip-top bag for storage. Keeps for up to 1 month in the fridge.

Baked Brie

7-inch wheel Brie (page 114)

1. Preheat oven to 200°F.

2. Place the fully-aged brie in an oven-safe mold approximately the same size and shape as the cheese (such as the mold that was originally used to shape the brie, if possible) and bake for 30 to 45 minutes, or until a thick rind develops on the surface.

3. Store in the mold with a tight-fitting lid. Keeps for up to 1 month in the fridge.

Herbed Cashew Cheese

MAKES APPROXIMATELY 4 CUPS

1 cup cashews, soaked and then drained

2 cups aquafaba

¾ cup coconut oil

½ teaspoon xanthan gum

½ teaspoon guar gum

¾ cup tapioca starch

¼ cup fresh basil

3 tablespoons nutritional yeast

2 tablespoons plus 2 teaspoons carrageenan powder

2 teaspoons tomato paste

2 teaspoons lactic acid

2 teaspoons onion powder

2 teaspoons salt

2 teaspoons fresh dill

1 ½ teaspoons turmeric powder

1 teaspoon garlic powder

1 teaspoon smoked paprika

1 teaspoon dried marjoram

¼ teaspoon dry mustard

¼ teaspoon black pepper

2 teaspoons apple cider vinegar

1. Combine the cashews and aquafaba in a blender and blend on high for 1 minute.

2. Whisk the coconut oil, xanthan gum, and guar gum together, add to the blender, and blend to combine.

3. Combine all the remaining ingredients except the apple cider vinegar, add to the blender, and blend to combine.

4. Transfer the mixture to a saucepan and place over medium-low heat. After 3 to 5 minutes the cheese will become lumpy from the tapioca; stir vigorously to achieve a glossy and smooth texture.

5. When the temperature reaches 170°F and the mixture is glossy with bubbles forming at the edges, remove from the heat and stir in the apple cider vinegar.

6. Pour the hot mixture into your preferred mold (silicone cupcake molds work great) and refrigerate for at least 4 to 6 hours, until set.

7. Store in the mold(s) with a tight-fitting lid, or transfer to a zip-top bag after setting. Keeps for up to 1 month in the fridge.

Cashew Cream Cheese

¼ cup coconut oil, safflower oil, or sunflower oil

1 tablespoon fresh lemon juice (about ½ lemon)

1 pint cashews, soaked and then drained

1 tablespoon maple syrup

1 ½ teaspoons fine sea salt

1 teaspoon black pepper

¼ teaspoon nutritional yeast

¼ teaspoon garlic powder

1. In a high-speed blender, combine the oil and lemon juice and blend on low.

2. With the blender running, stream in ½ cup water.

3. Turn the blender off and add all the remaining ingredients, then blend until whipped and smooth.

4. Store in a jar with a tight-fitting lid and refrigerate. Keeps for to 2 to 4 weeks.

BREADS AND BAKES

OPPOSITE, CLOCKWISE FROM TOP LEFT:
Key Lime Berries and Cream (page 324)
Elote (page 196)
Minty Rocky Road Ice Cream (page 325)
Avocado Pistachio Ice Cream (page 328)
Challah (page 135)

Bread is like dresses, hats, and shoes—in other words, essential!

—

Emily Post

Tortilla Wraps

MAKES 8 TORTILLAS

If you've never had fresh homemade tortillas, you are in for a treat. Nowadays, most restaurants don't make their own, but handmade tortillas are always worth the extra effort. These tortillas come together quickly, keep well, and can easily be converted into wraps, a taco bowl (page 123), or chips (page 124).

1 ½ cups all-purpose flour, and more for rolling

¾ cup fine cornmeal, and more for dusting

½ teaspoon salt

½ teaspoon garlic powder

Juice of 1 lime (about 1 ½ tablespoons)

Neutral cooking oil (safflower oil, sunflower oil, or avocado oil)

1. Mix all ingredients except the cooking oil together with 1 cup hot water, and let sit for 1 minute.

2. Dust a marble board or clean countertop with cornmeal. Transfer the mixture to the cornmeal-dusted work surface and knead 15 to 20 times, then let sit for 10 minutes.

3. Divide the dough into 8 parts. Roll each piece out on a flour-dusted work surface to a thin 6-inch round.

4. Heat the oil in a large cast-iron skillet over medium-low heat until very hot. Working in batches, add the tortillas and fry 2 to 3 minutes or until color deepens but doesn't brown, then flip and fry on the second side and repeat.

5. Use for tortilla wraps, or follow instructions below to use for taco bowls or tortilla chips.

6. Cooked tortillas keep up to 1 week in an airtight container at room temperature, and are best stored layered between sheets of wax paper.

PRO TIP: •

It's best to make the dough the same day that you intend to cook it, but it can be made 1 day in advance and stored overnight in the refrigerator, covered with a damp kitchen towel.

Tortilla Taco Bowls

Unlike the burrito bowls you may encounter at your local go-to grain bowl establishment, this adds an extra crunch, and a gorgeous presentation that will really deliver satisfaction. Usually reserved for Mexican family restaurants, the tortilla bowl is a bowl you can eat at the end or as you go, perfect for a no-waste picnic. If you opt for the large size bowls, divide the tortilla dough into 6 parts instead of 8 parts.

Neutral cooking oil (safflower oil, sunflower oil, or avocado oil)

8 small or 6 large Tortilla Wraps (page 121)

1. Preheat oven to 350°F.

2. Using 2 oven-safe tempered-glass nesting bowls, lightly oil the outside of the smaller bowl, and the inside of the larger bowl; the smaller of the two bowls should be slightly larger than the tortilla.

3. Lightly brush each tortilla with the cooking oil and place between the two oiled bowls, folding the edges of the tortilla to conform to the round shape of the bowls. Repeat with the remaining tortillas, working in batches if necessary.

4. Place the bowls open-side-down on a baking sheet and bake for 8 minutes.

5. Remove the outer bowls and bake 2 to 5 minutes more, until the tortilla bowls achieve the desired color and crispness.

6. Store in a large food container or zip-top bag at room temperature. Best used within 2 days, but keeps for up to 5 days.

Tortilla Chips

Fresh tortilla chips are really a treat, and what's better is that in this oven-baked recipe you control how much oil to use, and save on oil compared to deep-fried. I like to play with the seasonings when snacking with some salsa and guacamole, or keep it classic as below when making nachos, tortilla soup, or bringing them to a party. The recipe is the perfect solution to leftover tortillas, homemade or otherwise, and, in just a short time, will provide crunchy chips everyone will like.

8   still-soft (not crispy) Tortilla Wraps (page 121)

1   tablespoon neutral cooking oil (safflower oil, sunflower oil, or avocado oil)

1   teaspoon fresh lime juice

½   teaspoon salt

1.   Preheat oven to 350°F.

2.   Cut the panfried Tortilla Wraps into classic triangles or long rectangles (perfect for dipping) with a rolling cutter.

3.   Mix the cooking oil, lime juice, and salt together, and paint the mixture lightly over the cut tortillas.

4.   Spread out in an even layer on a baking sheet. Bake for 10 minutes, then flip and bake another 8 to 10 minutes, or until crispy and golden. Let cool.

5.   Best eaten immediately, but can be stored overnight in a food storage container lined with a paper towel.

PRO TIP: •

For a flavor boost, combine ¼ teaspoon neutral cooking oil, ¼ cup lime juice, and ¼ teaspoon salt in a spray bottle and lightly spray the tortilla chips while they crisp in the pan. Do not soak. This will keep the flavor strong in the oven, and help the crispness develop.

Blue Cornbread

Blue cornbread gets its charming color from a hearty heirloom variety of corn. Your local food co-op is the best place to locate blue cornmeal, but it is readily available on the internet as well. Don't be afraid to enhance the color with food coloring or blue spirulina and a slight underbake. This smoky maple-bacon cornbread can be served sweet or savory, and goes well with jalapeño jelly or paired with other smoky foods. See the photo of it on page 144.

Tempeh Crumble

4	strips tempeh bacon	2	drops liquid smoke or ¼ teaspoon hickory smoke powder
⅓	cup coconut oil		

Cornbread Mix

2	cups blue cornmeal, and more for coating	2	flax eggs (2 tablespoons ground flaxseeds mixed with 6 tablespoons warm water)
1	tablespoon cornstarch	1	tablespoon apple cider vinegar
1	teaspoon baking soda	1	tablespoon maple syrup
1	teaspoon baking powder	10	drops blue food coloring or 1 tablespoon blue spirulina (optional)
15	ounces Oat Milk (page 356)	1	tablespoon coconut oil

Glaze

2	tablespoons full-fat coconut milk (canned)	1	tablespoon maple syrup

For Serving

½	teaspoon smoked salt

1. Preheat oven to 375°F. Place a small pan of water at the bottom while it heats. This will create a humidity in the oven that allows a moister cornbread and reduces surface cracking.

2. In a 10-inch square cast-iron grill pan, cook the tempeh bacon in the coconut oil and liquid smoke until very hot and slightly crisp, 5 to 7 minutes.

3. Remove the tempeh and set aside. Drain the oil from the pan, but do not wipe out the pan.

4. Sprinkle cornmeal into the already-greased pan to lightly coat the bottom. Place the pan in the oven to warm it while you mix the batter.

5. Combine the cornmeal, cornstarch, baking soda, and baking powder in a large bowl. Combine the Oat Milk, flax eggs, apple cider vinegar, maple syrup, and food coloring, if using, in a separate bowl. Mix the wet ingredients slowly into the dry, then add the coconut oil, crumble in 3 strips of the tempeh bacon, and mix.

6. Let the batter sit for about 5 minutes, so the mixture can absorb the liquid. Remove the pan of water from the oven.

7. Transfer the batter into the hot pan and bake for 20 to 25 minutes.

8. Mix the coconut milk and maple syrup to create the glaze. Glaze the cornbread while still warm, and crumble the reserved tempeh strip on top.

9. Sprinkle smoked salt on top and serve.

10. Store at room temperature for up to 3 days wrapped in plastic wrap, or precut into servings and store in a glass food storage container.

PRO TIP: •
To reduce the crumbly texture, allow the cornbread mixture to sit and absorb the liquid thoroughly before baking. If the mixture looks too dry, add 1 tablespoon Plant Milk (page 33) and 1 tablespoon neutral cooking oil (safflower oil, sunflower oil, or avocado oil).

Sweet and Savory Scones

EACH VARIATION MAKES APPROXIMATELY 10 SCONES

Scones don't have to be the rock-hard lumps of flour you find in cafés. As the quintessential daytime entertaining food, they should be flaky, like buttermilk biscuits, and as soft as the gloves your grandmother might have worn while eating them at afternoon tea. Best eaten fresh, these scones are moist and flavorful and pair beautifully with butter or jam, or can be enjoyed on their own. Day-old scones work great cut in half for a breakfast sandwich or as a base for a Norwegian Benedict (page 171). Experiments with different fruits and herbs will not disappoint. Here are three variations to whet your baking appetite.

Strawberry Basil

2 tablespoons baking powder	2 tablespoons apple cider vinegar
1 ½ teaspoons salt	Vanilla extract (optional)
⅔ cup Cashew Milk (page 33) or Oat Milk (page 356)	1 cup freeze-dried strawberries
½ cup Homemade Butter (page 79)	2 tablespoons chopped basil
¼ cup maple syrup	3 cups all-purpose flour, or gluten-free all-purpose flour

Herbed and Spiced

2 tablespoons baking powder	¾ cup Cashew Milk (page 33) or Oat Milk (page 356)
1 tablespoon caster sugar	½ sweet onion, finely diced and sautéed
2 teaspoons arctic thyme or regular thyme	2 tablespoons fresh lemon juice (about 1 lemon)
1 ½ teaspoons salt	1 tablespoon jalapeño pulp
1 teaspoon crushed red pepper	3 cups all-purpose flour, or all-purpose gluten-free flour
½ cup Homemade Butter (page 79)	

Mole

1 tablespoon avocado oil

½ sweet onion, finely diced

½ teaspoon organic brown sugar

  Mole Paste (see below)

2 ½ tablespoons baking powder

1 ½ teaspoons salt

7 tablespoons Homemade Butter (page 79), and more, or cocoa butter, for brushing

¾ cup Cashew Milk (page 33) or Oat Milk (page 356), and more for brushing dough

3 cups all-purpose flour, or all-purpose gluten-free flour

Mole Paste

2 tablespoons cocoa butter, melted

2 tablespoons natural cocoa powder

1 tablespoon sesame seeds, toasted

1 teaspoon chipotle powder

1 teaspoon garlic powder

¼ teaspoon cayenne pepper, or more to taste

¼ teaspoon cinnamon powder

¼ teaspoon salt

¼ teaspoon black pepper

¼ teaspoon ground fennel

  Pinch clove powder

1. Preheat oven to 425°F, and place a baking sheet or marble board in the fridge.

2. For the Mole variation, begin by making the mole. Heat the avocado oil and cook the onion for 5 minutes, and then add the organic brown sugar and cook for another 3 minutes to lightly caramelize.

3. For the Mole variation, combine all ingredients for the Mole Paste, then mix with the caramelized onion and set aside.

4. For all scone variations: Mix together all the dry ingredients except the flour.

5. Mix together all the wet ingredients (including the mole for the Mole Variation), then slowly add the dry ingredients. Use a fork to combine these, because it comes together quickly, or a stand mixer on low.

6. Remove the chilled board from fridge and dust with flour.

7. Mix the dough until a firm ball forms, then flatten the ball to roughly half its original thickness. It should be the approximate surface area of 3 to 4 scones.

8. Cut as many rounds of dough as you can get out of the rolled-out dough, then re-roll the remaining dough, cut additional rounds, and repeat until all the dough has been used.

9. Transfer the scones to a baking sheet. Lightly brush the top of each one with more milk, or with a mixture of melted Homemade Butter or cocoa butter and milk.

10. Bake for 15 to 20 minutes, rotating once, then remove from the oven.

11. While best eaten fresh or the next morning, scones can be stored for up to 3 days in a cake-saver or a food storage container with a looser fitting lid, at room temperature.

PRO TIP: •

Underbaking will produce a sumptuous and moist scone; a longer bake will produce a toasty biscuit great for sandwiches and benedicts. Overworking the mix and adding a bit more flour will result in the lumpy scone you may be familiar with, especially if the dough is allowed to reach room temperature.

Paratha

Indian flatbreads are a good choice when you need fresh bread ready in a very short time. This paratha makes an excellent wrap, can be toasted into crackers, and pairs well with heavily sauced foods or charcuterie ensembles. The seeds add depth of flavor and texture, and different varieties of seeds can be substituted to suit additional flavor profiles as well.

1 teaspoon black mustard seeds

1 teaspoon cumin seeds

1 teaspoon ajowan seeds

3 tablespoons sesame oil

1 cup spelt flour or gluten-free flour (plus more for roller and board)

1 cup chickpea flour or whole wheat flour

1 ½ teaspoons salt

1 teaspoon smoked paprika

½ teaspoon cayenne powder or red chili powder

1. Toast the mustard, cumin, and ajowan seeds in a large frying pan over medium heat, tossing in the pan once or twice. Toast approximately 2 to 3 minutes, until fragrant.

2. Add the sesame oil and heat all together 1 to 2 minutes until hot. Remove from the heat and set aside.

3. Mix the spelt flour, chickpea flour, salt, paprika, and cayenne powder together, then slowly mix in ⅓ cup hot water. If the dough doesn't come together easily, add more hot water a tablespoon at a time.

4. Pour the sesame oil and seed mixture from the pan (use most or all the seeds and no more than 2 tablespoons of the oil) into the dough mixture, then return the pan to the stove.

5. While the oil in the pan reheats, mix the dough thoroughly. It should be moist with an elastic quality, but not sticky. If it is sticky, add more spelt flour.

6. Divide the dough into 9 balls and let sit 3 minutes.

7. Flour a marble board and a heavy roller with spelt flour. Roll out each ball to a flat, thin round with an even thickness of between $\frac{3}{16}$ inch and $\frac{1}{4}$ inch. Make sure there are no visible cracks or holes.

8. Turn the flame under the pan to medium heat to reheat the oil. Place each rolled-out dough circle into the pan and fry for 30 to 45 seconds per side.

9. Parathas can be kept warm in a different frying pan or a bain-marie over low heat.

PRO TIP: •
The oil in the pan is just to keep the dough from sticking on the first turn. A lighter touch with the amount of oil can help avoid a crispy cracker, though those can be delicious too, especially when you roll the dough extra thin like a popadum.

Challah

One of the most delicious and comforting breads, challah is traditionally made with eggs and a shiny egg wash. Here we use turmeric for a little color, potato water for a warm flavor, and a potato starch base for the wash. Challah is the perfect base for French toast, makes great sandwiches, and is vitally important to Jewish holiday meals. It is a complicated bread, with two rises—the temperature and timing of which are very important—and different weave options, but the results are worth the hard work.

3   Yukon Gold potatoes or other butter potatoes (about 1 ½ pounds), peeled and cubed

⅓   cup safflower oil or avocado oil

⅓   cup sugar

5   cups all-purpose flour or gluten-free all-purpose flour

1   tablespoon cornstarch

1   teaspoon kala namak (Indian black salt)

1   teaspoon turmeric powder

1   teaspoon sea salt

1   packet active instant dry yeast (approximately ¼ ounce)

½   cup Homemade Butter (page 79), softened and cut into small cubes

⅓   cup Oat Milk (page 356)

1. To make "potato water," combine the potatoes with 3 ½ cups cold water in a large pot, bring to a boil, and keep at a boil for 20 minutes, uncovered. The liquid level should reduce to about 2 cups.

2. Drain the potatoes, and reserve the liquid.

3. Combine 1 ½ cups of the potato water with the safflower oil and sugar in a mixing bowl or a large measuring cup with a pour spout (reserve the remaining potato water). Whisk until sugar is completely dissolved.

4. Combine the flour, cornstarch, kala namak, turmeric, and sea salt in a stand mixer and whisk to combine. Make sure there are no salt clusters for the yeast to come in contact with, then slowly add the yeast.

5. Change the mixer attachment to a dough hook, and slowly add the potato-water mixture to the dry ingredients while mixing. This slow pour should take about 1 minute.

6. Add in the softened butter, 1 cube at a time, until fully incorporated.

7. Knead using the dough hook on medium-high (number 6 on standard home machines) for 10 minutes, keeping an eye on the elasticity of the dough. Pinch and pull the dough to check its elasticity: When ready, it should stretch like a rubber band and reach about 10 inches without breaking.

8. Let the dough rise, covered, for 45 minutes at room temperature. It should double in size.

9. Portion the dough into 2 equal blocks. Divide each block into thirds to form a traditional straight braid, or into 4 sections to form a round braid. Roll the pieces into equal-sized ribbons that are at least 18 inches long. Line a baking sheet with parchment paper and braid the ribbons directly on the parchment, tucking the ends under and pinching them together.

10. Cover again and let rise a second time, for 30 to 45 minutes. The dough should dramatically increase in size, eliminating any gaps in the braid.

11. Preheat oven to 375°F.

12. While the bread rises, combine the remaining potato water (about ½ cup) with the cornstarch in a small saucepan. Bring to a simmer, whisk often until a thick gel forms, and then remove from the heat.

13. Slowly add the Oat Milk to the gel, whisking until the gel is thin enough to paint.

14. Brush a generous and even amount of the starch-and-oat-milk wash onto the risen bread right before placing in the oven.

15. Bake for 40 to 45 minutes, rotating once halfway through. Remove once the crust is smooth and dark and the bottom is strong. When you thump the bottom with your finger, it should sound hollow. The internal temperature should be 190°F to 200°F.

16. Paint the loaves again with more of the wash and let cool. Store in zip-top bags. Keeps for 3 to 5 days (if they last you that long!) at room temperature, or up to 6 months if frozen.

17. If you over-proof or let the finished loaves sit out uncovered or past 5 days and they get hard, it's French Toast time (page 149).

PRO TIP: ·
Save the boiled potatoes for one incredible potato salad. Combine with ¼ cup Cashew Dill Cream (page 82) and ¼ cup Cashew Cream Cheese (page 117) or Mayo (page 84), some chopped chives, ½ teaspoon paprika, ¼ teaspoon black pepper, and ¼ teaspoon salt, and throw in extra spices or diced celery to taste. Travels great!

Shortcrust

A versatile crust that can be used for practically any pastry, shortcrust can comprise both the top and bottom of pies and tarts. To form the ideal flaky crust, keep the fat cold and evenly distributed throughout the dough. Chilling all components will give you more time to roll and fold, contributing to the best flaky, melt-in-your-mouth texture. Remember to chill your filling before your final bake. To make this recipe gluten-free, use any all-purpose gluten-free flour blend and add ¾ teaspoon xanthan gum (instead of the usual ¼ teaspoon xanthan gum for every cup of flour).

2 ⅓ cups all-purpose flour

½ cup powdered sugar

Scant ¼ teaspoon salt

1 ¼ cups Homemade Butter (page 79), cut into ½-inch cubes, kept cold

1. Chill a roller, marble board, baking sheet, and 4 small tartlet pans in the fridge.

2. Sift the flour, sugar, and salt and mix together in a large bowl.

3. Cut the butter into the dry mixture using a pastry cutter.

4. On the chilled board, sandwich the dough between pieces of floured parchment paper or plastic wrap. Use the chilled roller to roll out to an even thickness, then fold in half and reroll at least once.

5. If making 4 tartlets, cut the dough into 4 pieces, otherwise use one flat piece. Press rolled dough into the chilled pans, pulling off the excess over the edges and using it to fill in any gaps or cracks as the dough conforms to the pan. Next puncture the dough heavily with fork tines. Make sure the dough is well ventilated, but don't completely split or fracture it.

6. Wrap each pan twice in plastic wrap, and freeze for 45 minutes.

7. Preheat oven to 350°F.

8. Place the pans straight from the freezer onto the chilled baking sheet and bake for 18 to 20 minutes, rotating halfway through.

9. Let cool before filling with the desired filling, or freeze the dough in the tartlet pans to use later. Keeps frozen for up to 1 month.

PRO TIP: . . . .

For larger pies or tarts or pies with creamy fillings, blind-bake (prebake) the crust with baking beans (or any large dry beans) and a few breathing punctures. This will create an even bottom and prevent bowing and cracking, which is especially important for large tarts, with diameters larger than 7 inches, or tarts with a wet filling. If your filling needs to bake for a long time (30 to 45 minutes), you can skip the prebake provided that the filling is not too wet. I usually prefer to prebake my crusts, prepare my fillings separately, and then combine for the final bake.

Coconut Tart Crust

Coconut flour is a gem for pastry baking. It takes well to liquid, combining quickly, and dries out easily, forming a crust that is as light and crumbly as it is strong, and there is no need to keep the butter cold or stress out about overmixing. This is a foolproof crust recipe and a real dietary skeleton key, being gluten-free, grain-free, and keto friendly in addition to delicious. Keep in mind, though, that a coconut-flour crust browns quickly and needs more liquid than your previous baking experience may lead you to believe.

½ cup soy milk or rice milk (or more, if dough is too sticky)

¼ cup coconut oil or Homemade Butter (page 79), melted, and more for greasing the pan

¼ cup liquid sweetener (like maple syrup)

¼ cup soft or silken tofu, drained

1 ½ teaspoons vanilla extract

1 tablespoon poppy seeds or seeds of choice (optional)

¼ teaspoon salt

1 cup coconut flour

¼ cup tapioca starch

¼ teaspoon lemon extract (optional, if dough is too sticky)

1. Preheat oven to 350°F.

2. Lightly grease one 8-inch tart pan or three 5-inch tartlets pans with the coconut oil and set aside.

3. Combine the soy milk, coconut oil, sweetener, tofu, vanilla, seeds, if using, and salt in a large mixing bowl. Mix until smooth.

4. Add the coconut flour and tapioca starch and mix by hand, kneading lightly until a tacky, soft dough forms. If the dough won't hold together in a firm ball and you're using poppy seeds, add the lemon extract; otherwise add more milk, 1 tablespoon at a time. Do not add so much liquid that the dough becomes wet or shiny.

5. Transfer the dough to the tart pan(s) and press down evenly, including into the base and up the sides.

6. Use a fork to pierce holes along the base of the crust to prevent bubbling while baking.

7. To blind-bake the crust for use with a baked filling, bake for 15 to 20 minutes. If no second bake will be required, bake for 25 to 30 minutes, checking and rotating every 10 to 15 minutes.

8. Remove from the oven and cool on a rack (in addition to cooling it more quickly, the rack will prevent the crust from getting dry and brittle). Make sure the crust and your filling are cool before assembling the tart.

PRO TIP: •
For those who wish to avoid soy, replace the tofu with ⅓ cup chickpeas blended smooth with your choice of Plant Milk (page 33), approximately ¼ cup, or as little as necessary to mix until combined.

Seed Crackers

MAKES 48 TO 64 CRACKERS

Bold, flavorful, and crunchy crackers packed with nutritious seeds could be a meal by itself. These crackers are delicious, but are also versatile enough that you could easily bring them along for a weekend hike, or make them a crunchy addition to your Charcuterie Board (page 265).

3 lemons	1 teaspoon cracked pepper
2 cups spinach	1 teaspoon cumin seeds
2 cups almond meal	1 teaspoon coriander seeds
¾ cup tahini	1 teaspoon black caraway seeds
⅔ cup ground flaxseeds	1 teaspoon dried oregano
⅓ cup chia seeds	½ teaspoon salt
⅓ cup nutritional yeast	
1 tablespoon sesame seeds	

1. Preheat oven to 375°F. Line a baking sheet with parchment paper.

2. Peel and squeeze out the juice from the lemons. Place the lemon pulps and all other ingredients in a food processor and pulse to combine. The mixture should not be wet.

3. Spread the mixture into a thin, flat, even layer on the prepared baking sheet. Wet your hands slightly and use them to smooth the surface.

4. Using a rolling cutter, cut even lines through the entire sheet to make 2-by-3-inch squares.

5. Bake for 35 to 40 minutes, rotating and flipping every 15 minutes, until crackers are completely dry and easy to lift off the parchment. Once they are liftable, snap them apart along the precut lines, remove the paper, and return the crackers to the baking sheet. Continue to bake until they brown and crisp thoroughly.

BRUNCH AND BREAKFAST

Brunch, for me, is an extended breakfast that should be enjoyed whenever you have time to properly engage in cooking and eating.

—

Yotam Ottolenghi

Madras Breakfast Taco

MAKES 2 TO 4 TACOS, DEPENDING ON DESIRED SIZE

This fun twist on the breakfast taco can be flavored and stuffed with a variety of ingredients. The combination of Indian spices with apples, currants, and leeks makes this a perfect winter brunch option that can help you diverge from the traditional blueberry pancakes and tofu scramble tacos you may have in heavy rotation.

1 tablespoon Madras curry spice

1 teaspoon sesame seeds or cumin seeds, toasted

2 teaspoons apple cider vinegar

Neutral cooking oil (safflower oil, sunflower oil, or avocado oil)

¼ cup chopped leek, and more, optional, for assembly

½ golden apple, diced, and more, optional, for assembly

2 tablespoons currants or chopped goji berries, and more, optional, for assembly

⅔ cup masa harina, and more to coat pancakes

Jalapeño Preserves (page 81) or Ibérico-Style Mousse (page 189), for assembly (optional)

1. Mix the Madras curry spice and sesame seeds in a heatproof bowl.

2. Boil ⅔ cup water and add to the spice-seed mix. Stir in the apple cider vinegar.

3. Heat the cooking oil in a sauté pan over medium heat, add the leek, apple, and currants and sauté until softened, then transfer to a bowl and set aside. Do not wipe out the pan.

4. Add the masa harina to the spice mixture and mix with a fork until doughy. Let stand 2 minutes.

5. You should be able to form balls from the dough. If not, add slightly more masa harina. Roll dough into 2 to 4 balls.

6. Dust sheets of parchment paper with masa harina, and place each dough ball between two sheets of parchment paper. Press hard to flatten; flatten as much as possible while still being able to lift the raw pancake in the air without it tearing.

7. Heat the sauté pan you used to cook the filling over medium heat. Add the masa harina tacos, in batches if necessary, and cook until gently browned on both sides, approximately 4 to 5 minutes per side.

8. Remove the tacos and fill with additional leeks, apples, currants, and Jalapeño Preserves.

PRO TIP: •
This recipe can also be used to create an omelet or crepe. To make an omelet or crepe, fill the masa harina while it's still in the pan so it crisps while you form it into your preferred shape. This also gives you a chance to warm the filling again and season the inside if salt or more spice is desired.

French Toast and French Toast Sticks

MAKE 4 TO 6 SERVINGS

Challah has the perfect richness and density for French toast, and two-day-old challah, or challah that didn't rise properly due to over- or under-proofing or underdeveloped gluten, makes amazing French toast sticks as soon as it cools. Either way you slice it, this recipe will inspire you to make more challah to reap the benefits. The addition of masala spice adds complexity to the typical cinnamon and cream flavors of French toast, but feel free to swap in pumpkin spice or keep it traditional. I like to serve this with the Jicama Hash (page 156) for a fusion of flavors that still resembles a standard American hearty breakfast.

Masala Chai Spice Blend

- ½ teaspoon green cardamom powder
- ½ teaspoon cinnamon powder
- ¼ teaspoon loosely packed saffron threads, crushed
- ¼ teaspoon black pepper
- ¼ teaspoon ginger powder
- ¼ teaspoon nutmeg powder
- ¼ teaspoon clove powder
- ¼ teaspoon vanilla bean powder (optional)

French Toast

- 1 banana
- 1 cup Flax Milk (page 33)
- 2 tablespoons all-purpose flour or gluten-free all-purpose flour
- 1 tablespoon ground flaxseeds
- 1 tablespoon maple syrup
- 1 teaspoon nutritional yeast
- 1 teaspoon cinnamon powder
- ¼ teaspoon nutmeg powder
- Pinch salt
- 1 loaf Challah (page 135), sliced or cut into sticks
- Homemade Butter (page 79), for frying

1. Combine all ingredients for the Masala Chai Spice Blend and set aside.

2. Mash the banana with a fork until homogenous.

3. Add the Flax Milk, all-purpose flour, ground flaxseeds, maple syrup, nutritional yeast, cinnamon, nutmeg, ½ teaspoon of the Masala Chai Spice Blend, and the salt and whisk together.

4. Dip the challah slices or sticks in the mixture to thoroughly coat both sides.

5. Heat the Homemade Butter in a frying pan over medium-high heat.

6. Fry the challah slices or sticks for 3 to 5 minutes on each side, until browned to preferred taste and texture.

> **PRO TIP:**
> For a truly decadent French toast, coat the challah in the batter, fry lightly, and then coat in batter and fry a second time, or even a third time—but no more than that! A fourth time is too decadent, even for me. The masala spice is a delicious variation on the classic French toast flavor, but can be omitted. Alternatively, save your extra masala chai spice for use in the Thai Chai Tea (page 360) or add it to any hot beverage of your choosing, such as coffee or back tea, about ½ teaspoon for a 12-ounce mug of tea.

Savory Crepelette

Many people refer to this dish as a chickpea omelet, but that has always seemed like a bit of a misnomer to me. Part omelet, part savory crepe, it combines the flavors, bite, and shape of an omelet with the crispy texture of a crepe. Cook longer for a more crepe-like texture, or slightly undercook for a moister, omelet-like mouthfeel. I like the filling below, but it's so versatile that it can be filled with a wide range of sweet or savory ingredients. Don't be afraid to dress with sauces like pesto, too.

Filling

¼ cup shiitake mushrooms, cut into strips	Salt and pepper, to taste
1 jalapeño or poblano chili pepper, sliced	¼ cup shredded fresh basil
½ red onion, thinly sliced	2 tablespoons Kimchi (page 101)
2 garlic cloves, chopped	2 tablespoons Mayo (page 84)

Batter

¾ cup Oat Milk (page 356)	¼ teaspoon onion powder
3 tablespoons Mayo (page 84)	¼ teaspoon turmeric powder
2 teaspoons apple cider vinegar	¼ teaspoon salt
¾ cup chickpea flour	¼ teaspoon baking powder
2 teaspoons nutritional yeast	¼ teaspoon chili powder
½ teaspoon kala namak (Indian black salt)	¼ teaspoon pink peppercorns, cracked, or more to taste
¼ teaspoon garlic powder	

For Frying

Neutral cooking oil (safflower oil, sunflower oil, or avocado oil)

OPPOSITE: Savory Crepelette and Purple Sweet Potato Pancakes (page 155)

1. Heat a sauté pan over medium-high heat. Add the mushrooms, jalapeño, onion, and garlic and sauté until tender. Season with salt and pepper.

2. Remove from the heat and mix in the basil and Kimchi.

3. Mix all ingredients for the batter together.

4. In a nonstick pan, heat a small amount of oil over medium heat.

5. Pour in the batter to form a thin round disc, like a pancake, and cook until the underside is golden and lifts with a spatula, then remove from the pan (do not flip). Repeat with the remaining batter.

6. Spread 2 tablespoons Mayo over each crepelette, fill with the sautéed vegetables, and fold over like an omelet.

PRO TIP: For an extra-filling omelet, replace ¼ cup of the chickpea flour with ¼ cup pea protein powder. For an extra-fluffy omelet, replace ¼ cup of the Oat Milk with ¼ cup whipped aquafaba.

Purple Sweet Potato Pancakes

MAKES 6 TO 8 PANCAKES

There is a potato pancake in nearly every culture. These nutrient-dense purple powerhouses make an excellent breakfast food, but could accompany any meal of the day, and certainly brighten up a fall or winter holiday party. The recipe can be made sweet or spicy, fruity or smoky, by increasing or decreasing some of the seasonings. You should also feel free to experiment with other seasonings and toppings.

2   tablespoons ground flaxseeds

2   skinny purple yams

1   red onion

1 to 2 bananas, depending on size (approximately ½ cup mashed)

1   tablespoon cumin powder

1   teaspoon cinnamon powder

1   teaspoon ginger powder

½   teaspoon salt

½   teaspoon black pepper, or more or less to taste

Neutral cooking oil (safflower oil, sunflower oil, or avocado oil)

1   strawberry, sliced, for garnishing (optional)

Cashew Sweet Cream (page 299) for garnishing (optional)

Fresh mint, shredded, for garnishing (optional)

½   cup apple preserves or applesauce for serving (optional)

1. Make 2 flax eggs by mixing the ground flaxseeds with 5 tablespoons water. Let sit.

2. Peel the purple yams and grate them using the wide holes of a box grater.

3. Grate the onion and mix into the yam. Squeeze the grated mixture to drain out excess liquid.

4. Mash the banana, then add the cumin, cinnamon, ginger powder, salt, and black pepper, and mash together with a fork until creamy. Combine with the flax eggs, and add to the grated mixture. Gently combine until mixed.

5. Coat a frying pan with just enough oil to coat completely, but not so much that the pancakes will be immersed in oil, and place over medium heat.

6. Press a small handful of the mixture flat between your hands to form each potato pancake.

7. Fry the pancakes in the hot oil until their surfaces look crisp, but are still purple, approximately 4 to 5 minutes each side. Once fried, place on a towel-lined plate, adding new, and hot, pancakes on top.

8. Garnish each serving with strawberry slices, a dollop of Cashew Sweet Cream, and fresh mint, and serve with apple preserves.

PRO TIP: . . . .

For extra-crispy pancakes, soak the grated yams in salt water for 20 minutes and drip dry in a sieve, then dry them with a towel before forming the pancakes.

Jicama Hash

MAKES 4 TO 6 SERVINGS

- 3 tablespoons ground flaxseeds
- 1 large jicama root (fist-sized in diameter), peeled
- 1 taro root, approximately 12 inches long, peeled
- 1 black radish
- 7 ½ ounces firm tofu
- 1 tablespoon apple cider vinegar
- 1 teaspoon toasted black sesame oil
- 1 green bell pepper, finely diced
- ¼ cup sesame seeds, toasted
- ¼ cup nutritional yeast
- 1 tablespoon garlic powder
- 2 teaspoons salt
- 1 teaspoon black pepper
- 1 teaspoon parsley flakes
- 1 teaspoon dried oregano
- ½ teaspoon cayenne pepper
- Neutral cooking oil (safflower oil, sunflower oil, or avocado oil)
- ¼ bunch green onions, chopped

1. Make 3 flax eggs by combining the flaxseeds with 8 tablespoons warm water. Let sit.

2. Shred the jicama, taro, and radish and soak them in salted water for about 8 minutes, changing the water once and re-salting.

3. Drain the shredded root vegetables and dry thoroughly using a clean tea towel or by letting drip-dry, then spread out to air-dry for 10 to 15 minutes.

4. In a blender, blend the tofu, apple cider vinegar, and black sesame oil into a smooth paste, then pour over the root vegetables and green bell pepper, and mix thoroughly.

5. Add the sesame seeds, nutritional yeast, garlic powder, salt, pepper, parsley, oregano, and cayenne pepper and mix, massaging with your hands.

6. Stir in the flax eggs and let sit for at least 3 minutes.

7. Heat the oil in a sauté pan or cast-iron skillet on medium-high heat. Add the vegetable mixture and heat, stirring for the first 5 minutes. Then add the green onions and let crisp undisturbed until the edges crisp, approximately 10 minutes.

PRO TIP: . . . .
You can also break the mixture into smaller pieces and serve it as a scramble.

Shakshouka

MAKES 6 TO 8 SERVINGS

Shakshouka is a traditional brunch everyone should be able to experience. This veganized version features slow-steeped vegan eggs baked in a red pepper and tomato stew. What's not to love? Watch the poached "yolks" spill their flavorful mixture out as the shakshouka cooks, resulting in a cheese-meets-egg texture and flavor. Choose between the molecular gastronomy spherizing technique that allows you to break the yolk over-easy style, or a modernist-kitchen-style formed yolk that stews as you cook. Be extra generous with the fresh herbs. A cast-iron pan is nonnegotiable for this dish.

Yolks

- 1 cup white glutinous rice
- 1 tablespoon Homemade Butter (page 79)
- ½ teaspoon yellow mustard powder
- 2 tablespoons nutritional yeast
- ½ teaspoon turmeric powder
- ½ teaspoon kala namak (Indian black salt)
- ¼ teaspoon black pepper
- ¼ cup refined coconut oil, melted
- 1 teaspoon toasted sesame oil
- 1 teaspoon alginate (optional, but needed for the molecular technique)

1. Rinse the rice 3 times, until the water runs clear, then combine it in a saucepan with 1 ½ cups water, the Homemade Butter, and the yellow mustard powder. Bring to a light boil, then reduce to simmer, and cook until the rice is completely soft, mushy, and gooey, and no liquid remains, approximately 20 minutes.

2. Combine the rice in a blender with all the remaining ingredients except the alginate and blend on high for 1 minute. If a breakable yolk is desired, add the alginate to the rice mixture and using a large 90-degree-angled soupspoon alginate, lower your yolk-sized portions into a calcium chloride bath. Remove your yolks after 30 seconds in the bath, and run under very gently running cool water, while still in the spoon. For a meltable, runny yolk, instead of a breakable yolk, use any neutral oil to grease semisphere molds (approximately eight to ten 1 ½-inch cups) generously, fill with the rice mixture (no alginate), and freeze for 2 to 3 hours. Remove from the molds and keep frozen until ready to cook.

Egg Whites

14 ounces firm tofu, in one block, drained	¼ teaspoon kala namak (Indian black salt)
1 teaspoon garlic powder	Neutral cooking oil (safflower oil, sunflower oil, or avocado oil)

1. Wrap the tofu in plastic or a freezer-safe bag and freeze for 30 minutes.

2. Remove the tofu and immediately slice lengthwise along its broad side to produce 5 or 6 thin slices.

3. Cut out one round or oval shape from each slice.

4. Combine the garlic powder and kala namak, and coat the tofu slices with the mix.

5. Heat plenty of oil in a frying pan over medium-high heat. Add the coated tofu and fry until the color of a fried egg appears on both sides, 3 minutes per side, twice, for approximately 6 minutes per side total.

Sauce and Veggies

3 tablespoons olive oil	2 teaspoons Harissa (page 31)
1 large red onion, one half diced and one half thinly sliced	1 teaspoon Berbere Spice Blend (page 31)
1 cup thinly sliced red pepper	½ teaspoon salt
4 garlic cloves, minced	¼ cup or more shredded parsley to garnish
2 ½ cups stewed tomatoes	
3 tablespoons red wine (I like a Mediterranean Barolo or rioja)	Paratha, toasted (page 132)

1. Heat the olive oil in a cast-iron pan over medium-high heat. Add the diced red onion and sauté until semitranslucent.

2. Add the red pepper and garlic and sauté for 3 minutes.

3. Add the stewed tomatoes and red wine and stir. Simmer for 3 minutes, then add the Harissa, Berbere Spice Blend, and salt and stir to mix.

4. Add the sliced red onion and the tofu egg whites, evenly spacing them throughout the pan with one in the middle.

5. Add the egg yolks on top of the tofu egg whites and spoon the tomato mixture over them. Cook until the eggs reach the desired runniness or temperature, 3 to 8 minutes depending on the method used and runniness desired. It's best to undershoot the time for breakable yolks or less runny eggs.

6. Sprinkle the parsley on top and serve straight from the pan, hot. Sop up the shakshouka with toasted Paratha.

PRO TIP: •
Cook everything with the egg whites first and add the yolks last in order to control the "breakability" of the yolk. Store-bought berbere can be used in place of the Berbere Spice Mix.

Quiche or Frittata

**MAKES ONE 10-INCH QUICHE OR FRITTATA,
OR 24 CUPCAKE-SIZED PORTIONS**

This recipe for this quiche or frittata (your choice) keeps well and travels well, making it a hit for brunch gatherings. It's delicious hot or cold and topped with fresh sliced vegetables and fresh herbs. The vegetables are interchangeable, allowing you to honor the seasons. The mixture lends itself to nearly any size and shape of baking dish, but it's best made in a 10-inch springform pan, or in individual portions in a cupcake pan to skip the headache of removing each slice. To make a frittata instead of a quiche, skip the crust altogether and proceed to the second part of the recipe.

Crust

1 tablespoon neutral cooking oil (safflower oil, sunflower oil, or avocado oil), and more for brushing	½ teaspoon cumin seeds
	Pinch salt
	1 tablespoon ground flaxseeds
1 ½ cups dry brown rice	

1. Heat the oil in the bottom of a 4-quart saucepan with a tight-fitting lid over medium-high heat, allowing the oil to coat the pan evenly as it heats.

2. Add the rice and cumin seeds and heat for 5 minutes, stirring often.

3. Add 3 ½ cups water and the salt and bring to a boil. Reduce the heat and simmer, covered, for 10 minutes.

4. Stir thoroughly, then cover again and cook for 20 to 30 more minutes, or until the water is completely absorbed.

5. Preheat oven to 375°F. Lightly grease a springform pan or cupcake pans with oil.

6. Remove the rice from the heat and let stand for 10 minutes.

7. Stir the flaxseeds into the cooked rice while warm but not hot.

8. Press the rice mixture evenly into the bottom of the prepared springform pan, and brush the top lightly with oil.

9. Bake for 15 minutes, or until set. Let cool in the pan while you prepare the rest of the ingredients.

Quiche Filling or Frittata

2 tablespoons safflower oil	½ cup Basic Broth (page 88)
3 red potatoes, diced	12 ounces firm tofu
1 small onion, diced	⅓ cup Flax Milk (page 33) or other nondairy milk (page 33)
8 ounces cremini mushrooms, chopped	
1 red bell pepper	2 tablespoons tamari or Soy-Less Sauce (page 77)
1 yellow bell pepper	1 tablespoon avocado oil
1 tomato, diced	⅓ cup nutritional yeast
3 scallion greens, sliced	2 tablespoons cornstarch
2 cups spinach	2 tablespoons ground flaxseeds
1 cup packed fresh basil	1 teaspoon kala namak (Indian black salt)
½ cup packed fresh cilantro	
¼ cup fresh oregano	1 teaspoon mustard powder
1 teaspoon crushed red pepper	1 teaspoon garlic powder
½ teaspoon salt	1 teaspoon cayenne powder
¾ teaspoon black pepper, divided	½ teaspoon turmeric powder

1. Preheat oven to 375°F.

2. Heat the safflower oil in a large sauté pan over medium-high heat. Add the potatoes and sauté for 5 minutes.

3. Add the onion and then the mushrooms, and cook, stirring often for 2 minutes.

4. Add the bell peppers, tomato, scallions, spinach, basil, cilantro, oregano, crushed red pepper, salt, ¼ teaspoon black pepper, and Basic Broth. Cook until the liquid reduces, stirring often.

5. Meanwhile, place all the remaining ingredients, including the remaining ½ teaspoon black pepper, in a food processor. Add 5 tablespoons warm water and blend until smooth.

6. When the liquid has cooked down in the vegetable mix, add the tofu mixture and cook, stirring to heat evenly, for 2 minutes.

7. To make a quiche, spoon the mixture into the prebaked crust and bake for 30 to 45 minutes depending on the depth of the pan, until the top is golden brown and the wobble is gone. To make a frittata, cook the mixture in a cast-iron pan over medium heat for 30 minutes stirring for the first 10 minutes and then letting cook undisturbed, then transfer to the oven for 15 to 20 minutes.

PRO TIP: •
The frittata can be made completely crustless in a muffin pan, and the mixture makes delicious mini muffins. They cook quickly and make a great quick bite at a brunch party or luncheonette. Alternatively, if you have a Shortcrust (page 138) or Coconut Tart Crust (page 140) premade in your freezer, it also works well in one of those.

Belgian Waffles

A classic stack of waffles is always a crowd-pleaser, and this gluten-free version ensures that everyone can enjoy them. The best waffles have a nice golden-crisp exterior and a moist, fluffy inside, which is best achieved with a generous half cup of the batter poured evenly on a hot iron and left to stand for 30 to 45 seconds before closing. Dust with powdered sugar and serve with Cashew Sweet Cream (page 299), fresh fruit, and maple syrup.

2 ¼ cups gluten-free flour (conventional all-purpose flour may be substituted; reduce by 2 tablespoons)

1 tablespoon sugar

1 ½ teaspoons baking powder

¼ tablespoon salt

1 cup room temperature Oat Milk (page 356) or Flax Milk (page 33)

1 ½ tablespoons melted Homemade Butter (page 79)

1 teaspoon vanilla extract

½ teaspoon apple cider vinegar

1. Mix the flour, sugar, baking powder, and salt in a bowl. In a separate bowl, combine the Oat Milk, Homemade Butter, vanilla, and apple cider vinegar, then slowly add the dry ingredients to the wet, whisking to combine.

2. Grease a waffle iron and preheat. Pour about ½ cup of the batter into the waffle iron and let stand for 30 to 45 seconds, then close and cook approximately 3 to 5 minutes. Gently open to check, adding an additional 1 to 2 minutes if needed. Repeat with the remaining batter.

PRO TIP: ·

Add freeze-dried berries, whole or powdered, or even blue spirulina or pitaya powder to get colorful waffles with fruity flavors and even a bit of crunch. Alternating colors of waffles is fun, nutritious, and festive.

Savory Baked Tofu Waffles

Kick off your day with a protein-packed savory winner that's just as good for lunch as it is for brunch. Any flavorful leaf can be used if you have trouble finding fresh shiso or sesame leaves; layered basil is also especially nice. Grains and sweets needn't dominate the breakfast and brunch food category.

14 ounces extra-firm tofu, sliced crosswise ½ to ¾-inch-thick (should yield 3 to 4 slices)

½ cup Basic Broth (page 88)

2 tablespoons tamari or Soy-Less Sauce (page 77)

1 tablespoon mirin or rice wine vinegar

1 teaspoon toasted black sesame oil

1 tablespoon finely chopped fresh cilantro

1 teaspoon garlic powder

½ teaspoon ginger powder

Shiso or sesame leaves, to taste

Grilled Red Pepper Sauce (page 75) or Cashew Dill Cream (page 82) for garnishing

Sesame seeds for garnishing

Kimchi (page 101) for serving

1. Press the tofu slices in between 2 salt blocks for 5 minutes.

2. Combine the Basic Broth, tamari, mirin, sesame oil, cilantro, garlic powder, and ginger powder in a bowl, and fully immerse the tofu slices in the marinade. Marinate overnight, or for at least 4 hours.

3. Preheat oven to 400°F.

4. On a baking sheet lined with parchment paper, bake the tofu for 35 to 40 minutes, flipping once halfway through, until the edges start to get crisp and dark. The tofu should look firm, dry, and more solid.

5. Heat a waffle iron and add a slice of the tofu. Press for 3 minutes, then and add shiso leaves. Press again to fuse the shiso leaves into the tofu and slightly crisp them, approximately 1 to 2 minutes. Repeat with the remaining tofu slices and leaves.

6. To serve, garnish the tofu with the sauces, sprinkle sesame seeds on top of each waffle, and serve with Kimchi.

PRO TIP: •
The baked tofu recipe is great for more than just waffles. Baked tofu is an excellent snack or sandwich filler, can be crumbled atop salads, and even makes an appearance in Pho Chay (page 209). It has a longer shelf life than uncooked tofu sitting in liquid, so make it ahead and keep it on hand for everything, including this savory breakfast food.

Norwegian Benedict

MAKES 4 EGGS WITH EXTRA YOLKS, ENOUGH FOR 2 TO 4 SERVINGS

This brunch classic presents the opportunity to flex your gourmet muscles. Combining freshly baked scones with a multistep egg, you'll master layered flavors that burst in the mouth and will craft a meal to impress even the most ardent omnivores at your table. Swap out the tomato for sautéed garlic and spinach for a Florentine Benedict.

Hollandaise

- 12 ounces soft or silken tofu
- ⅓ cup coconut oil
- 1 tablespoon nutritional yeast
- 1 teaspoon yellow mustard
- 1 teaspoon turmeric powder
- 1 teaspoon garlic powder
- 1 teaspoon onion powder
- 1 teaspoon salt
- ½ teaspoon kala namak (Indian black salt)
- ½ teaspoon black pepper
- ¼ teaspoon cream of tartar
- 12 ounces firm tofu
- 2 tablespoons extra-virgin olive oil
- ½ teaspoon garlic powder
- ¼ teaspoon kala namak (Indian black salt)
- ¼ teaspoon black pepper
- Pinch sea salt
- 1 white onion, sliced crosswise into thin rounds
- 2 to 4 Savory Scones (page 129)
- ½ cup mesclun greens for serving
- 4 to 8 pieces Smoked Salmon Lox (page 105), or more if desired
- Saffron or shredded red pepper for garnishing
- 2 tablespoons capers for garnishing
- Chives for garnishing

1. Combine all the hollandaise ingredients in a blender and blend until smooth, about 1 minute.

2. Divide the mixture in half. Reserve half in a serving dish at room temperature for the hollandaise sauce and transfer the rest to a saucepan to create the yolks.

OPPOSITE: Norwegian Benedict and Bloody Mary (page 350)

3. Slice the tofu block lengthwise to make 4 slices. Press the tofu slices in between 2 salt blocks to drain for 10 minutes.

4. Combine the extra-virgin olive oil, garlic powder, kala namak, pepper, and sea salt. Remove the tofu from the salt blocks and brush on both sides with the oil mixture. Refrigerate until ready for assembly.

5. Place the hollandaise in the saucepan over medium-low heat. Cook at a light boil, stirring often, to reduce the water and thicken, about 10 minutes. When the color deepens, pour the hollandaise into a semi-sphere silicone mold, with approximately 8 cavities if using a 1 ½-inch diameter cup.

6. Freeze the yolks in the mold for at least 2 hours. (They can be made ahead and kept, covered, for up to 2 weeks in the freezer.)

7. Transfer the yolks to the fridge 1 to 2 hours before cooking.

8. Heat a lightly oiled griddle or pan, add the onion slices, and sear for approximately 2 minutes per side.

9. Cut the tofu slices into round shapes using a large round mold, taking care to make slices that are at least 50 percent wider in diameter than the yolk semi-spheres, and approximately the same diameter as the scones.

10. Add the basted tofu to the griddle with the onion and sear, flipping once, until the appearance of a fried egg forms on both sides and it darkens at the edge.

11. While the tofu and onions sear, cut the scones in half and warm them on a frying pan, toasting lightly on both sides.

12. Layer the tofu, onion, Smoked Salmon, and yolks on each scone half to make open sandwiches, then cover with a tempered glass bowl to warm until the yolks reach the desired runniness.

13. Top with the saffron, capers, and chives, and serve with the reserved hollandaise sauce and a side of mesclun greens.

PRO TIP: •

To get a medium-runny egg, remove the yolk from the mold while it is frozen and thaw in the fridge for up to 2 hours, then prior to serving, add to the hot egg white while still on the griddle. For supremely runny, "over-easy" yolks, use either of the egg yolk methods from the Shakshouka recipe on page 159.

SMALL PLATES

OPPOSITE: Ceviche (page 179)

Seriously, if someone don't like this appetizer, you gotta grab they scruffy ass by the back of their neck and throw them out on the lawn. I can't help people like that.

—

Coolio
(from *Cookin' with Coolio*)

Pacaya Calamari "Palmamari"

MAKES 4 APPETIZER SERVINGS

The delightful texture and clustered form of pacaya makes it a natural choice for plant-based calamari. The flowers of this South American palm, which is also known as the date palm, have a neutral but slightly tangy flavor that picks up the marinade easily, and the crisp batter fry makes them a fun snack or appetizer for any game night or Italian meal. Serve with cocktail sauce and Cashew Dill Cream (page 82) for a flavorful bite. Look for fresh pacaya in Latin or Asian grocery stores, or if you're in a pinch, you can also usually find it preserved in glass jars in other grocery stores.

Marinade

- ¼ cup Onion Broth (page 88)
- ½ teaspoon tamari or Soy-Less Sauce (page 77)
- ¼ teaspoon blackstrap molasses
- 1 tablespoon powdered seaweed (I like to blend equal parts dulse, nori, and wakame)
- ⅛ teaspoon kala namak (Indian black salt)
- ¼ teaspoon flaxseed oil
- 16 ounces pacaya blossoms
- ¾ cup fine flour (rice flour or cake flour), or more as needed

- ¼ cup cornstarch
- 1 teaspoon baking powder
- 1 teaspoon salt
- ½ teaspoon sugar
- 1 cup gluten-free panko bread crumbs
- Approximately ½-gallon safflower or sunflower oil to fry
- Cocktail sauce for serving
- Cashew Dill Cream (page 82) for serving

1. Combine the Onion Broth, tamari, molasses, powdered seaweed, and kala namak. Divide the mixture in half and set one half aside.

2. Add the flaxseed oil to the remaining half and stir.

3. Drain the pacaya blossoms and dry well, then set them on a salt block, or a baking tray lined with parchment paper and a thin layer of sea salt for approximately 5 minutes.

4. Combine the pacaya with the flaxseed-oil marinade and marinate at room temperature for 1 hour.

5. Meanwhile, make a slurry with the other half of the marinade by adding the flour, cornstarch, baking powder, ½ teaspoon of the salt, and the sugar. Stir to mix, adding more flour as needed until you reach a thick, soupy consistency. Chill for 15 minutes.

6. Mix the panko bread crumbs with the remaining ½ teaspoon of salt.

7. Lift each pacaya piece out of the marinade and shoe off any excess liquid before you dip the pieces in the slurry and dredge them in the panko mixed with salt.

8. Fill a large pot with enough safflower oil to cover the pacaya pieces, and heat over medium heat until the oil reaches 350°F.

9. Fry each piece of pacaya in the oil for 2 to 3 minutes, or until crisp and slightly golden.

10. Remove fried pacaya with a slotted spoon and set on a rack over a drip pan while you fry the remaining pieces.

11. Serve with cocktail sauce and Cashew Dill Cream (page 82).

PRO TIP: ·
Heavy batter can obscure the tentacle texture of the palm, so keep the amount of batter light to maintain the visual appearance of the bumpy pacaya, which resembles the suckers on the tentacles of squid. You can also panfry the marinated pacaya and sprinkle with panko after.

Ceviche

Fresh, light, and bursting with citrus, ceviche is a bold tango of flavors on the tongue. Ceviche was one of those hard-to-give-up foods for me when I returned to the vegan fold. If you also miss the taste of ceviche, this will bring that range of flavors you probably thought you'd never experience again. If ceviche is new to you, prepare for your new favorite cold dish. Pair this light bite with freshly baked homemade Tortilla Chips (page 124) and the Tropicana Freeze (page 343), and it'll be like you're on the beach in Mallorca.

2 cups chopped artichoke hearts	1 tablespoon dried ground wakame
2 Roma tomatoes, diced	1 teaspoon dulse flakes
1 stalk celery, diced	⅛ teaspoon green spirulina
½ medium red onion, diced	⅛ teaspoon chlorella
¼ cup separated enoki mushrooms	Pinch kala namak (Indian black salt)
¼ cup chopped fresh cilantro, and more for garnishing	2 teaspoons Mayo (page 84) or Spicy Mayo (page 85) (optional)
2 large garlic cloves, crushed and minced	1 teaspoon red wine vinegar
½ medium jalapeño, diced	1 teaspoon fresh lemon juice
½ teaspoon salt, and more for garnishing	1 teaspoon maple syrup
	1 lime

1. Combine all ingredients except the lime and the garnishes. Add the juice of almost the entire lime, reserving a squeeze for garnishing, and toss together.

2. Refrigerate for at least 30 minutes.

3. Garnish with the remaining squeeze of lime juice, salt, fresh cilantro, and a slice or two of lime.

PRO TIP: •

Any vegetable is a welcome addition—just marinate first using the Fishy Marinade (page 86) and experiment. For a fun twist, try freshly squeezed orange juice instead of the lemon juice or lime juice.

Blistered Shishito Peppers and Smoked Carrots

MAKES 4 APPETIZER SERVINGS

Blistering peppers on the grill is one of my favorite ways to spend a summer night. If you're lucky enough to have a fire pit or an outdoor grill, you can cook the peppers on skewers to blister them quickly. Or use a cast-iron pan to create carefully placed grill marks for an embellished presentation. Keep the iron hot for the smoked carrots, a perfect partner for blistered peppers. Both of these can be made ahead, and also work well on snack plates, like the Charcuterie plate (page 265), featured separately or together.

Blistered Shishito Peppers

1 medium onion, roughly chopped into large chunks

8 to 10 cherry tomatoes, or more if desired

½ pound shishito peppers

2 tablespoons sesame oil

½ teaspoon sesame chili oil

1 ½ teaspoons sesame seeds

1 teaspoon nigella seeds

¼ teaspoon salt

1. Secure the onion chunks and cherry tomatoes onto skewers.

2. Heat a grill to high, or heat a cast-iron grill pan over high heat. Line up the shishito peppers in columns crosswise to the grill lines, then add the skewers to the grill.

3. Grill the peppers for 8 to 10 minutes, turning once, or until their skin blisters and black marks form in zigzags on their surface.

4. Remove the peppers from the grill and toss with the sesame oil, sesame chili oil, sesame seeds, nigella seeds, and salt.

5. Serve with the grilled onion chunks and tomatoes.

Smoked Carrots

1 cup hickory or applewood chips for smoking, or more or less as needed to cover bottom of Dutch oven

2 tablespoons tamari or Soy-Less Sauce (page 77)

½ teaspoon champagne vinegar

¼ teaspoon black sesame oil

¼ teaspoon hickory smoke powder

¼ teaspoon ginger powder

¼ teaspoon garlic powder

8 to 10 small carrots (purple and red work best)

Grilled Red Pepper Sauce (page 75) for serving

Nigella seeds for garnishing (optional)

1. Preheat oven to 375°F.

2. Add enough wood chips to a Dutch oven to thoroughly cover the bottom, and place in the oven to heat.

3. Combine the tamari, champagne vinegar, black sesame oil, hickory smoke powder, ginger powder, and garlic powder in a small saucepot and mix thoroughly.

4. Add the carrots to the mixture or transfer both carrots and marinade to a food storage container where they all fit. Marinate covered at room temperature for 15 minutes, making sure to turn them occasionally for even coverage.

5. Add carrots in marinade to the Dutch oven. Keep covered.

6. Smoke the carrots in the Dutch oven for 35 to 45 minutes, checking and turning every 15 minutes, until tender but not soft. (Your house will smell amazing.)

7. Heat a grill or cast-iron grill pan to high and transfer the carrots to the grill to finish cooking and create blackened grill marks, a crackly texture, and a savory char.

8. Serve over the Grilled Red Pepper Sauce and garnish with nigella seeds.

PRO TIP: •
Make sure the peppers are completely dry before grilling, otherwise they will blister without the flavor that comes from blackening. You can use tricolor baby carrots, but the best are the stubby, ugly heirloom varieties that come from the farmers market or are pulled straight from your own garden.

Escargot Amuse-Bouche

This new take on the widely adored French culinary classic is a rarity on modern menus, vegan or otherwise. Instead of the rich, buttery traditional presentation, this recipe amplifies the sea flavors, which contrast well with the sweetness from the raw watermelon, the umami from the seared watermelon, and the bright finish from the chive to provide a burst of flavor contrasts in a single bite. The dish is also a visual show-stopper, with plating that is a nod to other seafood presentations and a light seafoam that will show off your modern culinary prowess.

1   medium yellow watermelon

Fishy Marinade (page 86),
1 recipe portion

Dulse Foam (page 104),
1 recipe portion

Red watermelon, diced,
for garnishing

Chives for garnishing

Sea salt for garnishing

1. Cut the yellow watermelon in half and let the halves sit uncovered in the fridge for at least 4 hours, or overnight. The sections of watermelon will converge into small spiral-shaped clusters, typically about 3 per half of watermelon for a total of 6, although 8 is sometimes possible.

2. Remove the spiral-shaped sections of watermelon gently, using a spoon larger than the spirals to help preserve their delicate form, and place in a wide, shallow container. Reserve the remaining watermelon.

3. Add the Fishy Marinade to the spirals and marinate them at room temperature for 30 minutes.

4. Meanwhile, dice the remaining yellow watermelon and set aside for garnishing.

5. Heat a cast-iron pan over medium-high heat. Gently add the marinated watermelon spirals and sear, turning frequently, until a slight char develops and their color darkens.

6. Arrange each watermelon spiral in a small vessel, such as a duck spoon, and then top with approximately ½ to 1 teaspoon of the Dulse Foam so that the escargot beneath is still visible.

7. Garnish with diced yellow and red watermelon, chives, and a sprinkle of sea salt.

PRO TIP: •
Serve the duck spoons nestled on ice for a dramatic touch that nods to other seafood presentations, unless you can find a traditional French escargot plate. With a traditional escargot plate, skip the ice and dress the plate with the Dulse Foam before assembling your escargots, so they are nestled in seafoam. Crafty and thrifty home chefs can even craft "shells" from the watermelon rinds.

Fava Bean Tapas with Ibérico-Style Mousse

MAKES 4 APPETIZER SERVINGS

This tapas-style small plate combines smoked mousse and panfried fava beans with the liveliness of a Spanish flavor profile. I recommend plating with a bold-flavored jam such as the Spring Preserves (page 81) or Summer Preserves (page 81), so that notes of sweetness cut through the smoky intensity of the other components, allowing the layering of flavor on your tongue—salty, smoky, spicy, sweet, repeat. Enjoy this small plate on its own or as a side for a strong-flavored dish like Maitake Steak (page 271), and always dress with plenty of fresh aromatic garnishes.

Marinade

1 tablespoon apple cider vinegar	1 teaspoon Harissa (page 31)
1 tablespoon white dry cooking wine	½ teaspoon red chili flakes, or more to taste
1 teaspoon fresh lime juice	

Ibérico-Style Mousse

12 ounces firm tofu	1 teaspoon smoked paprika
¼ cup green grapes	½ teaspoon smoked salt (preferably alderwood smoked)
2 tablespoons blackstrap molasses	¼ teaspoon black pepper
2 tablespoons avocado oil	¼ teaspoon coriander powder
1 tablespoon roasted sesame oil	¼ teaspoon hickory smoke powder
1 tablespoon tamari or Soy-Less Sauce (page 77)	Pinch nutmeg powder

Other

¾ cup large fresh fava beans (from ½-pound whole pods)	Spring Preserves (page 81) or Summer Preserves (page 81) for plating
Neutral cooking oil (safflower oil, sunflower oil, or avocado oil)	1 sprig mint for garnishing
	Fennel fronds for garnishing

OPPOSITE: Maitake Steak (page 271) and Fava Bean Tapas with Ibérico-Style Mousse

1. Combine all the marinade ingredients in a large bowl and stir to mix. Add the fava beans, stir to coat with the marinade, cover, and let sit at room temperature for 45 minutes.

2. Combine all the mousse ingredients in a food processor and process until smooth, scraping down the sides to incorporate all ingredients.

3. Heat a frying pan over medium-high heat and add the neutral cooking oil to coat the bottom of the pan. Add the fava beans, discarding the marinade or saving it for up to 1 week for another use, and sauté until golden crescents are seared onto both sides, approximately 3 minutes per side.

4. Using the back of a weighted spoon, paint the mousse onto a serving plate, alternating with strokes of the sweet jam.

5. Place the fava beans on top of the painted sauces. Garnish with mint and fennel fronds.

PRO TIP: . . . .
Chill the mousse and jam before plating, and serve the beans piping hot on top, to enhance the dish's flavors.

Pâté-Stuffed Mushrooms

Savory finger foods can make or break a party, and these are so crave worthy that they can easily stand alone as their own meal. If full mouth bites of umami appeal to you or your guests, serve these pâté mushrooms stuffed with flavors inspired by the French feasts of the charcutiers that were as much about entertainment as they were about eating your fill (and often much more than your fill). Whether served as finger food, tapas, or a hearty side dish, this simple dish will be frequently requested at your house.

8 ounces medium cremini mushrooms (with caps larger than a silver dollar), stems removed and reserved for pâté	¼ cup balsamic vinegar
	¼ cup avocado oil
	Pinch salt

Pâté

1 cup walnuts, toasted	⅛ teaspoon lemon zest
Stems from 8 ounces medium cremini mushrooms, roasted	Pinch nutmeg powder
	Pinch salt
¼ white onion	Pinch black pepper
4 garlic cloves	1 tablespoon tamari or Soy-Less Sauce (page 77)
½ teaspoon dried tarragon	

1. Combine the mushrooms with the balsamic vinegar, avocado oil, and salt in a zip-top bag, seal, and let sit at room temperature for 30 minutes, flipping every 5 minutes.

2. Preheat oven to 350°F.

3. Combine all the pâté ingredients in a food processor and process until all ingredients reach a consistent small dice, the size of coarse sea salt.

4. Place the mushrooms open side down on a baking sheet lined with parchment paper. Roast for 12 minutes, flipping after 8 minutes.

5. To serve the pâté warm, remove the mushrooms, fill with the pâté, and return to the warm oven for 2 to 4 minutes. Otherwise, let the mushrooms cool, then fill with the pâté and serve at room temperature.

OPPOSITE: Pâté-Stuffed Mushrooms
and Sweet Potato Confit (page 194)

Sweet Potato Confit

Sweet and tender, a sweet potato confit is literally melt-in-your-mouth delicious. A true indulgence, it is best served in small portions, as a side or a small tapas-style appetizer, since it is fried at a low temperature for tenderness and richness. Confit is an excellent technique to treat vegetables, enriching the flavor and adding a creaminess to the texture, but was traditionally applied to salted meats to preserve them. It also works well applied to the Seitan Chicken (page 95) or Seitan Beef (page 96) recipes if you want a fattier and more tender texture.

2	cups Homemade Butter (page 79), or more as needed	1	small stalk lavender or 1 teaspoon herbes de Provence
1	sweet potato, cubed	1	whole dried chili pepper
1	sprig rosemary	2	garlic cloves, sliced
		1	green cardamom pod

1. Melt the Homemade Butter in a small saucepan on medium-low heat. Add the sweet potato cubes, and any additional Homemade Butter necessary to fully submerge the sweet potato.

2. Cover the pan and bring to a simmer, then uncover and add the remaining ingredients, stirring gently to mix and making sure not to bruise the sweet potato.

3. Simmer uncovered until the sweet potato is soft all the way through, approximately 30 minutes.

4. Best if served the same day, as the sweet potato will be too tender for a full reheat, although a slow reheat over a bain-marie will work if serving the next day, if refrigerated overnight in a food storage container with a tight-fitting lid.

Pearl Onion Confit

Unlike the sweet potato, the pearl onion transforms its flavor completely in the confit. The density of the onion reserves a little of the crunchy bite on the inside, while the outside browns and aromatizes into a savory treat unlike any other onion preparation you have had. You can cook them together if you scale up to a larger saucepan to give everything room to spread and if you want them to be flavored the same way, but add the onion in the last 12 minutes of the cook to ensure the balance of texture remains intact.

¼ cup Homemade Butter (page 79), or more as needed

4 garlic cloves, mashed

1 tablespoon red miso

1 cup pearl onions, peeled

1. Heat the Homemade Butter in a saucepan over medium heat.

2. Add the garlic and simmer in the melting butter, swirling together in the pan a few times, for 2 minutes.

3. Add the red miso and whisk vigorously to combine.

4. Once all the miso is dissolved, lower the heat to a light simmer.

5. Add pearl onions and cook, ensuring the butter covers the onions, and stir the mixture until the liquid is reduced by half, approximately 8 to 10 minutes.

6. Strain the garlic and onions, discarding the oil, and serve garlic and onions together.

PRO TIP: ·
Overcooked onions will result in a mushy dish. Save the butter and miso combo for sopping up with bread.

Elote

Elote is not just for food trucks. You can make this Mexican street corn at home, and it can be as simple or complicated as you desire—just be sure to consider the key elements of salt, fat, acid, and heat. I like to smoke the corn using my cast-iron grill pan in the oven, but if you have an outdoor grill the flavor is even better. Smoking the corn envelops it in a rich hickory flavor, and gets the kernels soft and juicy before slathering on the mayo, seasonings, and herbs. Don't hold back on the sauces: getting messy and licking your fingers is half the fun.

4 cobs fresh corn, halved	½ teaspoon garlic powder
1 tablespoon fresh lime juice	¼ teaspoon salt
2 cups hickory wood chips	¼ cup finely chopped fresh lemon basil for garnishing
½ cup Black Mayo (page 85) or Spicy Red Mayo (page 85), or a mixture of both	¼ cup cilantro leaves for garnishing
2 teaspoons Harissa (page 31)	¼ cup Cashew Cream Cheese (page 117) or Sour Cream (page 82) for garnishing
1 tablespoon nutritional yeast	Lime wedges for serving

1. Preheat oven, or grill, to 275°F. Place your wood chips in a cast-iron pan on the bottom rack, or in a pouch of heavy-duty aluminum foil with holes poked in it to let the smoke out.

2. Paint each piece of corn with the lime juice.

3. Smoke the corn cobs in a cast-iron grill pan if grilling in the oven, or place directly on the grill to sear grill marks onto each side by rotating every 15 minutes. Cook until tender and darkening in color, about 60 minutes.

4. Remove the corn from the grill, place each cob in a bowl for stability, and paint the mayo on. Be generous!

5. Mix the Harissa, nutritional yeast, garlic powder, and salt together and sprinkle the mixture over the corn.

6. Garnish each serving with lemon basil and cilantro, top with a dollop of Cashew Cream, and serve with lime wedges.

PRO TIP: ·

When coating the hot corn with mayo, setting it firmly in a bowl will hold it in place so that the mayo and seasonings don't slide off.

Papaya Salad

A proper Thai meal without a green papaya salad is practically unheard of, and with good reason. This invigorating small plate features tangy lime and crunchy peanuts that add to the sweet and savory notes and complement the spicy bites. Steer clear of the ground pork that many traditional variations have and instead, if you're feeling creative and adventurous, try adding some pan-toasted walnuts; crumble them and braise quickly in Porky Marinade (page 87) before toasting to fill them with flavor.

3 cups shredded green papaya	1 tablespoon Thai Spice (page 31)
½ cup slivered bamboo shoots	2 teaspoons demerara sugar
½ cup crushed peanuts, and more for garnishing	2 teaspoons ground dulse powder
10 green beans, chopped, and more for garnishing	1 teaspoon Himalayan salt
10 cherry tomatoes, chopped	1 teaspoon crushed red pepper
1 tablespoon grated fresh ginger	Juice of 1 lime (about 1 ½ tablespoons)
1 teaspoon chopped fresh Thai chilis	1 tablespoon tamari or Soy-Less Sauce (page 77)
2 tablespoons sunflower seeds, lightly toasted	1 head fresh iceberg lettuce for serving
2 tablespoons black sesame seeds, toasted	Flaxseed oil for serving
	Shaved carrot for garnishing

1. Combine the papaya, bamboo shoots, peanuts, green beans, tomatoes, ginger, chilis, sunflower seeds, sesame seeds, Thai Spice, sugar, dulse powder, Himalayan salt, crushed red pepper, lime juice, and tamari in a large mixing bowl and toss, then chill for about 1 hour.

2. Serve the chilled mixture over iceberg lettuce. Garnish with a drizzle of flaxseed oil, the shaved carrot, and more crushed peanuts and chopped green beans.

Green Quinoa Salad

What vegan cookbook would be complete without at least one quinoa item? Once the mainstay of vegan cuisine and health food menus everywhere, this complete-protein seed that blazed the trail of superfoods has mostly been left in the dust of other superfoods, and passed over with the increasing popularity of grain-free dishes. Nonetheless, quinoa is a delicious staple, and can add substance to a verdant salad—but please, seek out fair-trade sources.

Quinoa Mix

12 ounces white quinoa, rinsed and dried

1 tablespoon coconut oil

1 teaspoon whole coriander seeds

Pinch sea salt

Salad

3 cups spinach, hand torn

3 stalks celery, diced

1 stalk from a fennel bulb, diced

1 green bell pepper, diced

1 large cucumber, diced with skin left on

1 ½ avocados, diced

1 medium parsnip, peeled and diced

½ white onion, thinly sliced and chopped

½ cup chopped fresh cilantro

¼ cup chopped fresh Italian parsley

¼ cup chopped fresh dill

1 jalapeño, diced (with seeds if more heat is desired)

2 garlic cloves, crushed and minced

10 basil leaves, chopped

2 tablespoons sesame seeds, toasted

1 tablespoon freshly ground black pepper

Dressing

½ avocado

2 tablespoons extra-virgin olive oil

1 tablespoon fresh lime juice

½ teaspoon salt

¼ teaspoon ginger powder

1. Combine the quinoa and coconut oil in a saucepan over medium-low heat and cook, stirring, to gently toast until the color of the grain darkens slightly, about 2 to 3 minutes.

2. Add the coriander seeds, sea salt, and 4 cups room temperature water and bring to a boil, then reduce the heat, cover, and simmer for 10 minutes. Uncover and simmer for another 5 minutes.

3. Combine all the salad ingredients in a large bowl. Let the quinoa cool for 15 minutes, then add to the bowl and toss to help wilt the salad greens. Mix well.

4. Combine all the dressing ingredients in a blender and pulse to combine. Then transfer to a small mason jar or salad dressing bottle with a tight-fitting lid. Shake vigorously until it looks creamy, then toss with the salad.

5. Let cool at room temperature, then chill for at least 1 hour before serving.

Chef's Garden Salad

The vegetables in this salad are the ones I grow in my garden, and I like to encourage people to grow at least some of their own food. Learning about native plants, pollinator-friendly perennials, and our inefficient food system was very inspiring to me, and I made my small New England backyard an edible butterfly sanctuary. Whether you garden or not, this salad is a summer bounty of herbs and veggies that all come into season at the same glorious time, and give fresh textures and bright flavors for a salad that will defy your expectations of what a salad should taste like.

1 bunch lacinato kale	¼ cup Cashew Cream Cheese (page 117), whipped, and more (optional) for topping
2 cups spinach	
1 cup lamb's quarter	1 avocado, cut into wedges
½ cup fennel fronds and flowers	1 cup julienned watermelon
½ cup fresh dill fronds	1 tablespoon balsamic vinegar
2 English cucumbers, sliced	¼ cup chopped pecans, toasted
5 red radishes, sliced	1 tablespoon sprouted sunflower seeds
1 cup shredded carrots	
10 cherry tomatoes, quartered	Himalayan salt, to taste
½ jalapeño or 1 small jalapeño, diced	¼ cup crispy fried shallots, optional to garnish

1. Hand tear the kale, spinach, lamb's quarter, fennel fronds and flowers, and dill fronds and combine in a large bowl.

2. Add the cucumbers, radishes, carrots, tomatoes, and jalapeño and toss to combine.

3. Use a spoon to mix in the Cashew Cream Cheese.

4. Layer the avocado wedges and watermelon matchsticks over the top of the salad, alternating for color.

5. Lightly drizzle with the balsamic vinegar.

6. Sprinkle the pecans, sunflower seeds, and Himalayan salt over the top.

7. Top with shallots and a dollop more Cashew Cream Cheese, if using.

PRO TIP: •

Lamb's quarter, an edible weed prolific in the United States, is a hearty, dense green. It can easily be replaced by spinach or a mesclun mix if foraging is not your forte and your local farmers market has none on offer. Crispy shallots are best purchased to ensure a perfect crunch that lasts, but if you are interested in making them you should use them the same day they are made. To make crispy fried shallots, use equal parts thinly sliced shallots and a high heat oil, such as sunflower, and heat the oil in a small saucepan to about 275°F, adding the shallots to fry for about 7 or 8 minutes. Transfer to a dish towel to dry, raise the heat on the oil to about 350°F, and then lower the shallots in an angled and slotted frying spoon to let each fry for about 1 second. Be careful to not let them burn, and then immediately return each to the towel to drain.

Kale Chips

Oven-baked kale chips should be the new dinner rolls served before a meal. They are the perfect anytime snack that seems simultaneously like a salty snack and a health food. I have zeroed in on the exact ratio of heat and oil needed to get what I consider the perfect crunch-level, but feel free to dial back on the oil if you prefer; note though, that if you do this you may have to bake a little longer for that same crunch. Kale chips got me through many a long day thanks to the bodegas of Manhattan, but they are very expensive, and hallowed restaurants like Elizabeth's in Washington, DC, serve them as a waiting area snack before each seating. Now you can enjoy them anytime, and at a fraction of the cost.

Classic Kale Chips

- ¼ cup refined extra-virgin coconut oil (refined is necessary to avoid coconut flavor)
- ¼ cup nutritional yeast
- 2 teaspoons cumin powder
- 1 teaspoon Himalayan salt
- 1 teaspoon turmeric powder1 teaspoon cayenne pepper
- 1 teaspoon crushed red pepper
- ½ teaspoon coriander powder
- ½ teaspoon ginger powder
- ½ pound kale (curly or lacinato), stemmed

Tahini-Turmeric Kale Chips

- 3 tablespoons coconut oil
- 2 tablespoons tahini
- 1 teaspoon fresh lemon juice
- ¼ cup nutritional yeast
- 2 teaspoons garlic powder
- 1 teaspoon celery salt
- ½ teaspoon turmeric powder
- ½ teaspoon lemon pepper
- ½ pound kale, stemmed

1. Preheat oven to 275°F for the Classic Kale Chips, or 300°F for the Tahini-Turmeric Kale Chips.

2. Melt the coconut oil in a small saucepan over low heat. Remove from the heat and add all the remaining ingredients except the kale and stir to form a paste.

3. Thoroughly massage the mixture into the kale, making sure to cover every nook and cranny.

4. Spread the kale leaves on baking sheets lined with parchment paper. Make sure to spread evenly and avoid overlapping.

5. Place the sheets on the oven's middle rack and bake for 25 to 30 minutes, rotating the baking sheets every 10 minutes and flipping the kale once halfway through. Bake until crispy, but be careful not to burn. The Tahini-Turmeric Kale Chips may need to cook a little longer to achieve the same crispness, due to the added oils in the tahini.

PRO TIP: ·
Never try to make kale chips with wet kale. It is best to use kale that was washed the day before and dried overnight. Eat the chips immediately, or store in an airtight container lined with parchment paper.

SOUPS

OPPOSITE TOP: Potato and Leek Sous Vide Soup (page 222)
OPPOSITE BOTTOM: Cucumber Soup (page 217)

I live on good soup,
not fine words.

—

Jean-Baptiste Molière

Pho Chay

Few things satisfy quite like a bowl of noodle soup. In pho chay, anise, clove, and cinnamon round out the savory broth by adding a touch of sweetness and complexity. The vegetable elements are not set in stone, so you may substitute to your taste, as long as the vegetables you choose have a good satisfying bite that allows the warm, flavorful broth to flirt with your taste buds for as long as possible. Thinly sliced Seitan Beef (page 96) would not be out of place, nor would King Oyster Scallops (page 244). Enjoy the aroma lingering in your kitchen for hours after cooking. It has the power to make you, and everyone around you, instantly hungry.

1 tablespoon sesame chili oil, and more as needed

1 teaspoon tamari or Soy-Less Sauce (page 77)

½ teaspoon ginger powder

14 to 16 ounces drained peppered konjac noodles or fresh flat rice noodles (use banh pho noodles if you prefer a standard pho)

Pho Broth (page 90), 1 recipe portion

½ pound baby bok choy

1 cup trumpet mushrooms

½ cup bias-cut sliced rice cakes

8 ounces Baked Tofu (page 168), sliced

2 sticks burdock root, slivered

6 sliced rounds pickled radish

4 ounces bamboo shoots, slivered

Black sesame seeds for topping

1 bunch fresh basil for topping and serving

Bean sprouts for serving

Gochujang or sriracha (optional) for serving

1 lime wedge for serving

PRO TIP: •

If fresh rice noodles can't be found, use 16 ounces cooked dry flat rice noodles.

1. Heat a large sauté pan or wok over medium heat. Add the sesame chili oil to coat, then add the tamari, ginger powder, and peppered konjac noodles, cutting the noodles with kitchen scissors as you add them to the pan. Toss the noodles to coat in the oil and seasonings, and heat for approximately 4 to 5 minutes, tossing occasionally throughout.

2. Place the noodles in a large soup bowl and fill the bowl halfway with the Pho Broth, keeping the noodles centered. Return the now-empty sauté pan to the heat.

3. Pull the leaves of the bok choy apart, add to the pan, and sauté until tender.

4. Remove the bok choy and place on one side of the soup bowl.

5. Add the trumpet mushrooms to the sauté pan. Cook for 3 minutes, then add the rice cakes and more sesame chili oil to help sear, an additional 2 minutes on each side.

6. Place the mushrooms, rice cakes, tofu, burdock, radishes, and bamboo shoots around the bowl. Top with the black sesame seeds and basil, and garnish with more sesame chili oil. Serve with bean sprouts, fresh basil leaves and florets, hot sauce, and a lime wedge on the side.

PRO TIP: ....

To go the extra mile, marinate the mushrooms and bamboo shoots in the Beefy Marinade (page 86) or Porky Marinade (page 87) overnight before incorporating, and drizzle the leftover marinade into the sauté mix at the end. You can also add smoked salt or Chinese Five-Spice Powder (page 29) to the baked tofu marinade to boost its taste even further.

Watermelon Gazpacho

MAKES 4 TO 6 SERVINGS

Bright and refreshing, this summer soup is cool, sweet, and tangy. The watermelon balances out the traditional tomato, imparting a steady natural sweetness that plays against the garlic and red onion. Serve with a big spoon and enjoy the hydrating properties.

3 cups chopped watermelon, plus 1 slice for garnishing

1 large heirloom tomato

2 stalks celery

¼ cup red onion

4 garlic cloves

2 scallion greens, roughly chopped

Zest of ¾ lime, and remaining lime peel for garnishing

¼ cup avocado oil, and more (optional) for garnishing

1 teaspoon red wine vinegar

Pinch salt

Pinch black pepper

1. Combine all ingredients, except the garnishes in a food processor, and process until the desired thickness is reached.

2. Transfer the mixture to a large serving bowl and chill in the fridge for 2 hours.

3. Cut the reserved watermelon and lime peel into thin strips.

4. Divide the gazpacho among soup bowls, and garnish each serving with the watermelon and lime peel strips and a drizzle of avocado oil.

PRO TIP: •

Let the gazpacho sit, covered, in the refrigerator overnight in step 2 if you have the time. The flavors will develop best with time.

Sunchoke-Celery Root Soup

MAKES 4 TO 6 SERVINGS

Sunchokes are the chimera of the late summer garden. They look a bit like sunflowers on top, and the root, the part you eat, looks a bit like an ancient potato, but they taste a bit like an artichoke, hence their second name: the Jerusalem Artichoke. Celeriac, also known as celery root, has an earthy flavor that combines flavors similar to parsnip and celery and is a delight in creamy applications, as with this soup. Together, sunchokes and celeriac are my favorite summertime root vegetables, and this soup has them dancing together on your tongue.

6 to 7 cups Onion Broth (page 88)

1 pound sunchokes, peeled and quartered

1 pound celery root, peeled and chopped

1 sweet potato, scrubbed and diced

1 teaspoon safflower oil or avocado oil, and more to toss

Pinch salt

1 bunch scallions, chopped, keeping the green and white parts separated

½ to 2 garlic cloves, crushed and minced

1 teaspoon matcha powder

1 teaspoon coriander powder

½ teaspoon celery salt

½ teaspoon dried tarragon

¼ teaspoon black pepper

1 tablespoon Homemade Butter (page 79)

1 tablespoon fresh lemon juice (about ½ lemon)

1 avocado, chopped

Pepita Garnish

¼ cup pepitas, and more for garnishing

½ teaspoon avocado oil

½ teaspoon smoked paprika

¼ teaspoon salt

¼ teaspoon rubbed sage

Black pepper, cracked, for serving

Scallions, sliced, for serving

1. Preheat oven to 425°F.

2. Heat the Onion Broth in a soup pot, covered, over medium heat for 5 to 6 minutes.

3. Toss the sunchokes, celery root, and sweet potato in the safflower oil and season with pinch of salt. Spread onto a baking sheet and roast for 30 to 40 minutes.

4. Reduce the heat of the Onion Broth to low and simmer, covered, simmering until the root vegetables are done.

5. Remove the root vegetables from the oven, add to the pot with the simmering broth, and continue to simmer, covered, for 15 more minutes.

6. Meanwhile, reduce the oven temperature to 350°F and make the pepita garnish.

7. Toss the pepitas with the avocado oil, smoked paprika, salt, and rubbed sage. Spread onto a baking sheet and toast for 10 minutes, or until dry.

8. During the broth's last 5 minutes of cooking, add the white parts of the scallions, garlic, matcha powder, coriander, celery salt, tarragon, black pepper, and ½ tablespoon Homemade Butter, then add the lemon juice and avocado.

9. Using an immersion blender, blend the soup until even and smooth. Add the remaining ½ tablespoon butter for an extra rich and creamy taste, if desired.

10. Divide the soup among bowls and top each serving with the pepita garnish, black pepper, and green parts of the scallions.

Cucumber Soup

Keep cool on a summer day with a big bowl of this refreshing soup, or remember summer when the season is over with late-harvest cucumbers. Be careful not to over-blend or you'll end up with a light, fluffy mousse, but don't fret too much if you do—it will settle down and lose some of its air in the fridge. This soup is as good for the skin as it is for the stomach, and with this combination of ingredients you'll keep your electrolytes balanced all through backyard-barbecue season. See the photo of it on page 206.

1 cup Coconut Milk Yogurt (page 103)	1 cup packed fresh lemon basil, and more for garnishing
2 large cucumbers, roughly chopped	¼ cup packed fresh mint
2 avocados, pitted and skin removed	1 teaspoon apple cider vinegar
2 stalks celery, roughly chopped	1 teaspoon garlic powder
2 scallions, chopped, 1 reserving sliced white parts and 1 for garnishing	1 teaspoon salt
	½ teaspoon black pepper
	Smoked paprika for garnishing

1. Combine all ingredients except the garnishes in a blender and blend to combine. For a thinner or smoother consistency, add water, 1 tablespoon at a time, until desired thickness is reached.

2. Best if chilled before serving for at least 2 hours, but can be eaten at room temperature.

3. Divide among soup bowls and garnish each serving with a line of smoked paprika, sliced white scallions, and basil.

French Sorrel Soup

I fell in love with the piquant French sorrel leaf as a young child. My mother grew it, which is fortunate since it can be tricky to find raw outside of farmers markets and French gourmet shops. She made a simple sorrel soup for me, and still always has some waiting for me when I come home for a visit. While this recipe is much heartier than the simple creamy lettuce soup my mother makes, it is an homage to the zesty green soup of my childhood and brings forward that tangy sorrel boldness that made me fall in love with it as a kid.

2 tablespoons safflower oil

1 Spanish onion, diced

3 medium Yukon Gold potatoes, diced

¼ cup plus 1 tablespoon Homemade Butter (page 79)

7 cups chopped sorrel (with stems), plus 3 cups chiffonade

6 cups Basic Broth (page 88)

5 scallions, sliced, keeping the green and white parts separated

3 garlic scapes, finely diced

1 cup canned light coconut milk, at room temperature

3 tablespoons finely chopped fresh cilantro, or more sorrel

2 tablespoons fresh lemon juice (about 1 lemon)

1 tablespoon garlic powder

1 tablespoon black pepper

1 teaspoon fine sea salt

Pinch citric acid

1. Heat the safflower oil in a six-quart soup pot over medium-high heat, then add the onion and potatoes. Cook, stirring often to prevent sticking, until soft, about 8 minutes.

2. Add ¼ cup Homemade Butter, and stir until melted.

3. Add the chopped sorrel and cook to wilt gently, then add the Basic Broth.

4. Add 2 of the sliced scallions to the soup pot, reserving some of the green slices for garnishing, and add the garlic scapes.

5. Once the broth is warm, after about 2 to 3 minutes, add the room temperature coconut milk, and bring to the same temperature, approximately 2 minutes.

6. Combine the remaining 3 scallions with two-thirds of the chiffonaded sorrel and the cilantro and set aside, ready for use in step 8.

7. Raise the temperature of the soup just enough to get a light bubble, then turn the heat to low.

8. Add the garlic powder, black pepper, sea salt, and citric acid to the soup and mix thoroughly, then add the sorrel-scallion-cilantro mixture and the remaining tablespoon of Homemade Butter.

9. Heat for 3 more minutes, then remove from the heat, let cool, and transfer to the refrigerator to chill.

10. Serve chilled, topped with the remaining sorrel chiffonade and green sliced scallions.

PRO TIP: ·

For a less creamy soup or to avoid the use of coconut milk, substitute 2 tablespoons Homemade Butter (page 79), ¼ cup Cashew Cream Cheese (page 117), or ½ cup Plant Milk of your choice (page 33) for the coconut milk.

Portion out servings and store in the fridge so you are less tempted to eat it all in one sitting. Or is that just me? The flavors become amazing after a night in the fridge.

Mongo Guisado

A comfort-food staple of the Philippines, this soup can be made with sea flavors or pork flavors depending on your mood. Either way, the soup's ample portions burst with aromas. When the temperature dips and all you want to do is cozy up inside, this restorative soup will take your winter blues away.

Mung Beans

¼	pound mung beans	2	whole cloves
1	garlic clove, crushed	1	black cardamom pod
1	tablespoon whole cumin seeds	½	teaspoon kala namak (Indian black salt)
1	teaspoon yellow mustard seeds	¼	teaspoon black pepper
½	teaspoon salt		

Tofu

¼	cup tamari or Soy-Less Sauce (page 77)	1	teaspoon powdered mushrooms (preferably shiitake or maitake)
2	tablespoons avocado oil or sesame oil		Pinch chardonnay oak–smoked salt
2	tablespoons Thai Spice (page 31)	14	ounces firm tofu, chopped into 1-by-2-inch blocks
2	tablespoons powdered wakame		

Fish Cakes

½	cup bias-cut sliced rice cakes		Pinch citric acid
1	tablespoon crushed wakame	1	bay leaf

Soup Base

1	large or 2 medium sweet yellow onions	1	heirloom beefsteak tomato, diced
4	garlic cloves	1	cup mustard greens
1	tablespoon sesame oil	4	cups Onion Broth (page 88)
1	whole habanero pepper, finely diced	1	tablespoon Thai Spice (page 31)
		¼	cup chopped fresh cilantro
			Rice (optional)

1. Combine the mung beans, garlic, cumin seeds, mustard seeds, salt, cloves, and cardamom with 6 cups water in a soup pot. Cover and bring to a boil, and then cook uncovered for 30 to 40 minutes. When tender, add the kala namak and black pepper, mash lightly, and set aside.

2. While the mung beans are still boiling, combine the tamari, avocado oil, Thai Spice, wakame, powdered mushrooms, and chardonnay oak–smoked salt with ¼ cup water. Add the tofu and marinate at room temperature until the beans are done, about 30 minutes.

3. Rehydrate the rice cakes in 2 cups hot or boiling water with the wakame, citric acid, and bay leaf.

4. On a salt block, dice the yellow onion and mince the garlic. If not using a salt block, sprinkle a pinch of salt on the cut onion and garlic before adding them to the pot.

5. Heat the sesame oil in a small soup pot on medium heat and add the yellow onion. Cook, stirring often, until translucent, then add the garlic and habanero and cook for 1 minute.

6. Add the marinated tofu in its marinade and sauté for 5 to 7 minutes on each side, or until the surface starts to turn golden.

7. Drain the rice cakes, and add them,the tomato, mustard greens, and 1 cup of the Onion Broth to the pot, and heat together for 2 minutes, stirring once or twice.

8. Add the remaining 3 cups Onion Broth and the Thai Spice and bring to a light boil. Slowly stir the mung bean mixture in, 1 large spoonful at a time.

9. When the mixture reaches a consistent temperature, remove it from the heat and stir in the cilantro.

10. Serve over rice.

PRO TIP: •
Spinach can be used in place of the mustard greens, and seitan in place of the rice cakes. For a thicker soup, blend the beans in a blender with the broth and add together in step 8.

Potato and Leek Sous Vide Soup

The slow, low, evenly distributed heat of cooking sous vide is an incredible way to develop a complex soup. In this soup, the long, slow extraction allows for the leek flavor to open fully, aided by the warm fat of olive oil—an excellent oil for a low-heat cook. The cashew-based cream sauce gives this country classic the feel of a chowder, but any of the other cream sauces in the book can be substituted if you have them on hand.

Soup

12 cups diced Yukon Gold potatoes	1 teaspoon cumin powder
5 cups leeks, white parts removed	1 teaspoon salt
¾ cup minced garlic	½ teaspoon fennel seeds
4 sprigs oregano, whole leaves only	½ teaspoon black pepper
5 whole fresh sage leaves	4 cups Basic Broth (page 88)
4 fresh bay leaves	1 cup extra-virgin olive oil
2 teaspoons smoked paprika	

Cream Sauce

⅔ cup cashews, soaked and then drained	½ teaspoon fresh lemon juice
⅔ cup Onion Broth (page 88)	¼ teaspoon salt
½ cup Cashew Milk (page 33)	Pinch black pepper
¼ cup maple syrup	Chives for garnishing

1. Set a sous vide machine to 165°F.

2. Combine all the soup ingredients in a vacuum-sealed bag or a zip-top bag using the water immersion method (page 317), and place the bag in the sous vide machine. Weigh the bag down to keep it fully submerged.

3. Cook at 165°F for 1 ½ to 2 hours, until potatoes are tender.

4. Meanwhile, combine all ingredients for the cream sauce in a high-speed blender and blend until smooth. Transfer to a glass jar or squeeze bottle and refrigerate.

5. When the potatoes are tender, remove the soup bag from the sous vide and open the bag carefully. Transfer the contents to a large, heatproof bowl and add ½ cup of the cream sauce.

6. Use an immersion blender to mix in the cream sauce and break down the vegetables, blending just until the soup is combined but still chunky.

7. Serve garnished with the chives and more of the sauce.

MAINS

OPPOSITE, CLOCKWISE FROM TOP LEFT:
Flan (page 333)
Polenta Pissaladière (page 285)
Lasagna Skyscrapers (page 277)
Squid Ink with Black Bean Pasta (page 291)
Polenta Tian (page 281)

Today's innovation is tomorrow's tradition.

—

Lidia Bastianich

Sunday Roast

Brined and marinated over several days, this slow roast combines the sweetness of watermelon with the smoky flavors of a Christmas ham or roast beef, and is more than worth the careful planning. The sugars from the watermelon form a skin, which will char slightly—just like a traditional roast. The marinated watermelon is juicy, savory, and sweet and will melt in your mouth; the longer it sits in the marinade, the deeper the flavor and juicier the roast will be. And because of its resemblance to a traditional roast, your guests will definitely do a double take when this centerpiece reaches the table.

Brine

2 quarts Onion Broth (page 88)	2 heads of garlic, peeled and crushed
6 cups Porky Marinade (page 87)	1 cup salt
1 ⅓ cups Beefy Marinade (page 86)	1 teaspoon hickory smoke powder
1 cup brewed coffee	1 medium watermelon, rind removed and one side scored
¼ cup balsamic vinegar	4 bulbs garlic, peeled, cloves kept whole but separated
¼ cup toasted black sesame oil	2 onions, roughly chopped
1 teaspoon liquid smoke	2 long sprigs rosemary, leaves only

1. In a large food-safe container with a tight-fitting lid (such as a 22-quart foot prep and storage container), mix 4 quarts water and all the brine ingredients together. Place the watermelon inside, making sure the liquid covers the top, and weigh down the watermelon with plates to keep it submerged. Cure for 2 or 3 days at room temperature and away from direct sunlight, or longer depending on the desired flavor and juiciness. Keep the watermelon submerged the whole time.

2. Preheat oven to 450°F.

3. Remove the watermelon from the brine, and discard the brine. Place the watermelon on a roasting pan with the scored side up and cover with foil. Roast on the center rack of the oven with the watermelon centered for 20 minutes, so the scored top gets a crosshatched look like a roast.

4. Roast the watermelon for another 30 minutes, this time uncovered, and turned over to allow it to baste it in its own runoff juices. Turn again, and roast for another 30 minutes, then turn the watermelon on one end, allow to baste again, and continue roasting for 20 more minutes.

5. Turn the watermelon onto its other end, adding the garlic, onion, and rosemary to the pan and basting again, and roast for 20 minutes.

6. Turn again, this time placing the crosshatched side up, and baste one more time. Roast until a strong brown skin forms on the top and the entire watermelon is firm, approximately 20 minutes.

7. Remove the watermelon from the oven and let stand for 10 minutes before cutting and basting one last time.

> **PRO TIP:** · · · · · · · · · · · · · · · ·
> Roasts are often stuffed with herbs and garlic, and that isn't a bad strategy here, but be careful of the fragile quality of a raw watermelon. Try to stuff aromatics into preexisting holes from any seeds.

Temaki and Sushi Party

MAKES 8 TO 10 SUSHI ROLLS AND UP TO 24 TEMAKI HAND ROLLS

Sushi is a wonderful way to eat a lot of fresh and cooked veggies, one delicious mouthful at a time. Sushi rolls, sashimi pieces, hand rolls (temaki), and onigiri make attractive platters for a cocktail party. An assemble-your-own temaki party is also a fun way for your guests to create an edible bouquet: just prepare all ingredients, pre-roll some temaki, and encourage your friends and family to make their own combinations.

Sushi Rice

1	cup black rice	1	teaspoon organic fine sugar
1	cup fine white sushi rice	½	teaspoon salt
1	teaspoon mirin		
1	teaspoon rice vinegar		

1. Rinse the black rice and fine white sushi rice thoroughly, then combine with 3 cups water in a saucepan over medium-high heat. Bring the water to a boil, then lower the heat to a simmer, cover, and cook for 20 minutes.

2. In a separate small saucepan, combine the mirin, rice vinegar, sugar, and salt and cook over low heat, stirring often, until the sugar dissolves.

3. When the rice is finished cooking, let stand 5 minutes, then slowly pour in the liquid mixture, stirring gently with a wooden spoon, and fluff. The rice is best made and served once cooled to room temperature, but can be made ahead and stored in a well-sealed food storage container with a damp cloth spread across the top.

Baked Avocado Tempura

2 avocados

½ cup almond flour

½ cup chickpea flour

½ cup cornmeal

1 tablespoon tapioca starch

1 teaspoon nutritional yeast

1 teaspoon salt

½ teaspoon smoked paprika

¼ teaspoon black pepper

⅔ cup Flax Milk (page 33)

1 teaspoon fresh lemon juice

1 tablespoon mixed milled flaxseeds and chia seeds

½ teaspoon garlic powder

½ teaspoon cumin powder

Panko bread crumbs for coating

1. Heat oven to 375°F.

2. Slice the avocados into even wedges, making approximately 8 wedges per avocado.

3. In a medium bowl, combine the almond flour, chickpea flour, cornmeal, tapioca starch, nutritional yeast, ½ teaspoon of the salt, the smoked paprika, and the black pepper.

4. In another medium bowl, combine the Flax Milk, lemon juice, flaxseed-chia seed mix, garlic powder, cumin powder, and remaining ½ teaspoon salt.

5. Pour the panko bread crumbs into a third medium bowl.

6. Toss the avocado wedges in the flour mix, then carefully dredge in the wet mixture, allowing excess liquid to drip off. Coat completely with panko bread crumbs.

7. Place the coated avocado wedges on a baking sheet lined with parchment paper.

8. Bake for 10 minutes, then carefully flip, making sure to leave the coating intact. Continue baking another 5 to 7 minutes, until crisp and golden. Best served same day; use immediatley or keep at room temperature until ready to serve.

Lotus Root Tempura

Sesame oil or a blend of safflower oil and sesame oil, as needed

½ cup tapioca starch

1 tablespoon ground flaxseeds

½ teaspoon black pepper

½ teaspoon kala namak (Indian black salt)

¾ cup rice milk

4 ounces Lotus root, sliced and cut into strips or half moons

Panko bread crumbs for coating

1. Heat 1 inch of sesame oil in a small, straight-sided sauté pan with a lid. Bring the temperature to approximately 325°F for a shallow fry.

2. Mix the tapioca starch, ground flaxseeds, black pepper, kala namak, and rice milk together in a medium bowl, whisking vigorously to introduce many air bubbles. Pour the panko bread crumbs into another medium bowl.

3. Submerge the lotus root in the tapioca batter, allowing it to coat every hole, and letting any excess batter drip off.

4. Coat the battered lotus in the panko bread crumbs.

5. Submerge the lotus pieces in the sizzling sesame oil and panfry until crispy, about 1 minute on each side.

6. Transfer the fried lotus to a paper towel–lined plate to absorb some of the oil.

7. Let cool at room temperature, and enjoy within 2 hours of cooking.

Caviar

1 cup Seaweed Tea (see below)	**Optional Color:** ¼ teaspoon spirulina for green, ½ teaspoon activated charcoal for black, ½ teaspoon paprika for red, or 3 drops of food coloring for any other desired colors
1 ¼ teaspoons sodium alginate	
½ teaspoon calcium lactate	

1. Combine the Seaweed Tea, sodium alginate, coloring, if using, and blend with an immersion blender to mix well.

2. Strain the mixture through a sieve into a clean vessel, and let sit for 10 to 15 minutes.

3. Mix the calcium lactate with 2 cups water in a wide bowl. Stir until the calcium lactate is dissolved to make a receiving bath, and set up a large bowl with cool water and set aside.

4. Using a syringe, spherification spoon, or spherizer (recommended for beginners), slowly drip the Seaweed Tea mixture into the receiving bath, one drop at a time. Let each drop sit for 1 minute, then remove gently with a slotted spoon and place immediately into the bowl with cool water.

PRO TIP: ·
Vegan caviar is a fun technique with many applications beyond sushi. You can make flavorful pearls that literally burst with flavor for many applications from cocktails and desserts to salads and more.

Seaweed Tea

¼ cup wakame	2 tablespoons dulse flakes
1 teaspoon sea salt	1 teaspoon flaxseed oil
¼ teaspoon kala namak (Indian black salt)	

1. Combine the wakame, sea salt, kala namak, dulse flakes, and 2 cups water in a small saucepan over medium-low heat and simmer for 15 to 20 minutes. Do not boil.

2. Remove from the heat and strain through a sieve.

3. Stir in the flaxseed oil.

4. Can be made up to 1 week in advance and kept in a jar with a tight-fitting lid in the fridge.

PRO TIP: ·

Any 1 cup of flavored liquid, low in acidity, will work in place of the seaweed tea

To Assemble Temaki and Maki Rolls

Nori sheets or soy sheets	Bamboo shoots
Sushi Rice (page 231)	King oyster mushrooms or enoki mushrooms, baton sliced and marinated in Fishy Marinade (page 86)
Spicy Red Mayo (page 85)	
Smoked Salmon (page 105)	
Baked Avocado Tempura (page 232)	Wasabi paste
Lotus Root Tempura (page 233)	Tamari or Soy-Less Sauce (page 77)
Arugula sprouts	Sesame seeds (optional)
Yellow pepper strips	Caviar (page 234) for garnishing

For Temaki Rolls

1. Cut the nori sheets into thirds to create long rectangles. Holding the left side of one nori rectangle in the palm of your left hand, cover your palm area, approximately one-third of the sheet, in 3 tablespoons cooked Sushi Rice.

2. Using wet fingers or a large spoon, spread the rice into a flat, even layer. Add a dollop of Spicy Red Mayo, some wasabi, or a sprinkle of sesame seeds.

3. Working in a diagonal from the base of your pinkie to the base of your thumb, across your palm, start to build your roll. Place one or two pieces of your desired filling onto the nori, curving your palm slightly to cup and shape the roll.

4. Fold the bottom left edge of the nori sheet from the heel of your palm diagonally over and up toward the base of your index finger, maintaining good tension on the nori as you fold.

5. Continue to roll the sheet toward your thumb, twisting tightly, so the bottom becomes a cone.

6. Seal the last corner of the sheet with a mashed piece or two of rice and smooth shut.

7. Garnish with Caviar, if using.

For Maki Rolls

1. Cover a bamboo mat in plastic wrap, and place a full sheet of nori on top.

2. Center 1 scant cup of sushi rice on the bottom half of the nori sheet (closest to you) and spread evenly, stopping just 2 inches short of the far edge.

3. Layer your desired ingredients horizontally, keeping them approximately 1 inch away from the edge of the rice line in all directions. Add Spicy Red Mayo, wasabi, or tamari, if using.

4. To roll the sushi, start by folding the bamboo mat away from you and curling it inward to make a tight spiral. Continue to roll in a spiral all the way to the opposite side, squeezing gently with your fingers to maintain tension.

5. When completely rolled, encase the sushi in the bamboo mat and roll on the table one or two times to compress and seal completely.

6. Remove the sushi roll from the bamboo mat and store, wrapped in plastic, in the fridge, or remove from the plastic and cut into roughly 8 pieces.

7. When completely rolled, encase the sushi in the bamboo mat and roll on the table one or two times to compress and seal completely.

PRO TIP: •
Rolled, uncut sushi keeps best. Wrap in plastic wrap and then in parchment paper and store in the fridge for up to 2 days, and cut just before serving. Dipping your knife in a bit of cool water between cuts makes it easy to cut the sushi roll into pieces, but make sure to not cut the sushi with a soaking wet knife.

Moules Frites

Moules frites is a bistro classic that can make any gourmand's mouth water. With corn, potatoes, polenta, and huitlacoche, this recipe shows off the versatility of your vegan-cuisine tool kit. Huitlacoche has a rich and complex flavor, and when combined with the artichoke the texture emulates that of mussels and the sight will trick the eye. The delicious truffle corn has a musky, complex flavor that comingles with the deep flavors of the marinade for a surprising multifaceted effect. Different textures and flavors from mushroom to sea come together sumptuously in this visually delightful dish. Expect many questions from the curious foodies at your table about this one.

Mussel Shells

1 tablespoon avocado oil	6 purple potatoes
¼ teaspoon salt, or more for extra crispness	

Garlic White Wine Sauce

4 tablespoons Homemade Butter (page 79)	4 white garlic cloves, minced
½ cup dry white wine	1 tablespoon masa harina or dry polenta
3 Black Garlic cloves (page 107)	Sea salt, to taste
4 shallots, 2 minced and 2 thinly sliced	Fresh parsley for garnishing

Assembly

½ cup Spicy Red Mayo (page 85)	Flaxseed oil to drizzle (optional)
2 tablespoons wakame, rehydrated in cool water	Pinch sea salt (optional)
5 marinated artichoke hearts, leaves pulled apart	Polenta Fries for serving (optional, page 240)
⅓ cup huitlacoche, marinated overnight in Fishy Marinade (page 86)	Potato Wedges for serving (optional, page 241)

1. Preheat oven to 425°F.

2. Mix the avocado oil and salt together.

3. Cut the potatoes in half lengthwise, so their oval shapes are emphasized. If an extra-crispy crust is desired, soak the potatoes in salted room temperature water for 15 minutes (note, though, that soaking may lighten their color).

4. Using a butter knife, trace the edges of the natural visible lines in the flesh of the potatoes. Score to separate the potato flesh from the outside, leaving a very thin amount of flesh to strengthen the peel. Use a spoon to remove each hemisphere of flesh in one piece, and set aside for potato wedges (page 241).

5. Paint the inside and outside of each hollow potato shell with the mixture of avocado oil and salt, then place the potatoes hollow side down on a baking sheet lined with parchment paper.

6. Bake until crisped and strong, 35 to 45 minutes, flipping twice. The edges should be slightly brown and lighter than their original color. Let cool, long enough to handle, on the baking sheet.

7. Meanwhile, make the sauce. Melt the Homemade Butter and combine it in a blender with the white wine and Black Garlic. Blend until mostly smooth.

8. Transfer 2 tablespoons of the mixture to a small saucepan over medium heat. Add the minced and sliced shallots and the white garlic, and sauté for 3 minutes.

9. Add the remaining butter mixture, bring to a simmer, and reduce the heat to low.

10. Add the masa harina and cook, whisking, for about 3 minutes to thicken.

11. When the mixture has thickened to the desired texture, remove from the heat. Add the sea salt.

12. Transfer to a serving dish or gravy boat and garnish with fresh parsley.

13. After the purple potato skins have cooled, add a dollop of Spicy Red Mayo and a piece of rehydrated wakame to each potato skin.

14. Remove the largest leaves from the artichoke hearts, and then place 1 tender leaf from inside the open artichoke heart in each potato skin.

15. Inside each artichoke leaf, place another dollop of Spicy Mayo, followed by a piece of huitlacoche, followed by another smaller artichoke leaf, leaving some of the huitlacoche exposed.

16. Drizzle with flaxseed oil and sprinkle with sea salt. Serve with Polenta Fries and Potato Wedges.

Polenta Fries

Prepared Polenta from Scratch (page 109)	1 teaspoon crushed red pepper
	½ teaspoon garlic powder
Olive oil (in a mister or spray bottle)	½ teaspoon dried basil
¼ cup masa harina or fine polenta flour	¼ teaspoon fine sea salt
	¼ teaspoon black pepper

1. Preheat oven to 450°F.

2. Cut the prepared polenta into 3-by-½-by-½-inch sticks.

3. Mist lightly with the olive oil.

4. Combine all the remaining ingredients in a small bowl, and roll the polenta sticks in the mix to coat.

5. Place the sticks on a parchment-lined baking sheet, leaving ample room around each. They should not touch.

6. Bake for 40 minutes, flipping once halfway through, or until all edges are slightly crisped. For extra-crisp fries, after baking, lightly mist again with the oil and broil on low for 1 to 2 minutes.

Potato Wedges

- 2 large russet potatoes (skin kept on), cut into 8 or more wedges
- 4 cups salt water (4 teaspoons salt dissolved in 4 cups of water)
- ¼ cup avocado oil
- 2 sprigs fresh rosemary, leaves stripped off and chopped
- ½ teaspoon salt
- ½ teaspoon ground black pepper
- ½ teaspoon cumin powder
- ½ teaspoon onion powder
- ½ teaspoon garlic powder

1. Preheat oven to 450°F .

2. Soak the potato wedges in the salt water for 15 minutes, then remove and pat down with a dish towel to dry thoroughly. Let stand on a clean dishrag for 2 to 3 minutes to further air-dry.

3. Combine the avocado oil with all the remaining ingredients, then toss the potato wedges in the mixture to coat.

4. Place the wedges on a baking sheet lined with parchment paper, evenly spaced so that none are touching.

5. Bake the wedges for 25 minutes, flipping after 10 minutes. The wedges should be tender but crispy on the outside, and slightly golden at the edges. To make them extra-crisp, broil on low for 2 to 3 minutes after baking. Do not add more oil.

PRO TIP: ·
If huitlacoche is too much trouble to find, canned straw mushrooms are an okay stand-in, but I recommend ordering the huitlacoche for the wow factor.

King Oyster Scallops with Glazed Grilled Endive and Radicchio

MAKES 10 TO 15 SCALLOPS, DEPENDING ON SIZE OF MUSHROOMS;
ENOUGH FOR 2 SHAREABLE PLATES

Plating is easy when your ingredients are beautiful, and the king oyster scallops and orange-glazed endive and radicchio make the process simple and fun. Meaty textures, sweet orange bursts, and savory grill flavors combine to make a great bite. This dish is ideal for sharing from one plate, tapas-style.

Marinade

¼ cup tamari or Soy-Less Sauce (page 77)

1 tablespoon flaxseed oil

1 teaspoon rice wine vinegar

¼ teaspoon blackstrap molasses

1 teaspoon dulse flakes

1 teaspoon wakame powder

¼ teaspoon kala namak (Indian black salt)

Stems from 2 to 3 large king oyster mushrooms, cut into rounds approximately ½ inch thick

Glazed Grilled Endive and Radicchio (page 245) for serving

1. Combine all the marinade ingredients in a bowl and whisk by hand until aerated and the color has lightened uniformly. Do not use a hand mixer.

2. Place the mushroom stem rounds into a wide, flat casserole dish or other shallow dish (not a bowl). Spoon the marinade over the stems, being careful to only expose the tops and bottoms (the cut sides) to the marinade. Marinate for 30 minutes, flipping once.

3. Heat a flat cast-iron pan over high heat until water droplets travel from one end of the pan to another immediately when added. Add the mushroom stems and pan sear each side for 2 to 3 minutes, drizzling on the remaining marinade in between flips for added flavor, until the sides begin to caramelize and an even sear across the surface is achieved. Do not overcook.

4. Serve with the Glazed Grilled Endive and Radicchio.

Glazed Grilled Endive and Radicchio

4   clementines, 3 juiced and 1 sectioned for serving

2   tablespoons maple syrup

¼   teaspoon white miso paste

6   small or medium-sized Belgian endives, halved

6   robust pieces of red radicchio

Neutral cooking oil (safflower oil, sunflower oil, or avocado oil)

Fresh thyme leaves for garnishing

1. Whisk the clementine juice, maple syrup, and white miso paste together in a small bowl until the paste is completely dissolved.

2. Paint the mixture onto the endive and radicchio pieces, coating the cut sides generously and allowing some paste to penetrate the layers. Reserve the remaining glaze.

3. Heat a grill or cast-iron grill pan on medium heat with a very light amount of the neutral cooking oil. Grill the endives, first on the uncut sides and then on the cut sides, allowing fine black grill marks to sear into the cut surfaces, usually about 2 minutes on each side.

4. Flip the endives and add the radicchio next to them. Pour the remaining glaze mixture over the endives and radicchio pieces, and grill for another 2 to 3 minutes, stopping just before the radicchio starts to go from purple to brown.

5. Garnish with thyme while still on the heat and leave for 1 minute more. Remove, using tongs to preserve the juices, when the radicchio's color starts to fade.

6. Serve with the sectioned clementine.

PRO TIP: •

Grilling on cast iron gives an extra dimension of flavor and it's worth using in this recipe, unless you can grill outdoors over robust wood chips.

Winter Cornucopia Squash Bowl

This is a homey meal that uses seasonal root vegetables, cold-weather leafy greens, and warming nuts. Deep savory flavors with a sweet maple finish are perfect for winter, and the natural squash bowl does the decorating for you. You can serve the extra squash seeds on the side or snack on them while cooking.

2 large acorn squash	¼ cup maple syrup, and more for garnishing
2 tablespoons avocado oil, and more to paint the squash	2 parsnips, chopped
1 teaspoon cinnamon powder, and more to dust	1 bunch lacinato kale, stemmed and chopped
¼ pound pecans, chopped	½ teaspoon cumin powder
¼ pound walnuts, chopped	½ teaspoon smoked paprika
1 white onion, diced	¼ teaspoon salt
4 garlic cloves, minced	

1. Preheat oven to 425°F.

2. Cut both squash in half from tip to stem. Remove seeds and loose pieces, and scrape down the sides. Transfer the seeds to a bowl of water to make separating them from the fleshy parts easier.

3. Paint the insides of the squash with avocado oil and dust with cinnamon. Place the squash cut side down on a baking sheet and cook for 25 to 35 minutes, until the flesh can be easily penetrated with a fork.

4. Meanwhile, toast the chopped nuts in a large sauté pan over medium-low heat for 3 to 5 minutes, until lightly golden and starting to give off a lightly pleasant aroma.

5. Add the 2 tablespoons avocado oil to the pan, then add the white onion. Sauté until the onion becomes translucent, then add the garlic and sauté for 1 minute.

6. Add the maple syrup and parsnips and sauté until tender, about 8 minutes. Then add the kale and cook until it appears vivid green. Remove the mixture from the heat.

7. Finish cleaning the reserved seeds and dry them with a clean kitchen towel. Combine the 1 teaspoon cinnamon and the cumin, smoked paprika, and salt and toss the seeds in the mixture. Transfer to a baking sheet.

8. When the squash is done roasting, remove it from the oven and reduce the temperature to 400°F. Toast the nuts in the oven for 10 to 15 minutes, or until crispy.

9. Fill the roasted squash halves with the sautéed ingredients, and sprinkle with the seeds. Return to the oven for 5 to 10 minutes to set. Drizzle with maple syrup before serving.

PRO TIP:

Serve with Mulled Cider (page 359) or Buttered Brandy (page 352) to further the seasonal feel. If the squash isn't stable on its own, place it in a ceramic bowl for support.

Savory Caramelized Onion and Bean Tart

MAKES ONE 10-INCH TART, ENOUGH FOR 8 SERVINGS

Make this tart ahead of time and have it ready for the next time you're playing effortless host, or show up to the next gathering with this flawless bake. Satisfying and visually impressive, this savory tart will disappear in even less time than it took for you to make it. The Shortcrust (page 138) it calls for, used for several recipes in this book, may become something you make ahead and freeze raw or parbaked, allowing you to always have a bakery-perfect dish ready to pull out of the oven. Don't hold back on the edible herb and tomato garnishes for a stunning display.

Shortcrust dough (page 138)

Caramelized Onions

2 tablespoons Homemade Butter (page 79)	¼ cup fresh basil
4 medium sweet onions, thinly sliced	1 tablespoon maple syrup
2 cloves fresh garlic, minced	1 teaspoon balsamic vinegar
	½ teaspoon salt

Filling

1 can pinto beans (approximately 15 ounces)	¼ teaspoon salt
1 can cannellini beans (approximately 15 ounces)	¼ teaspoon crushed rosemary, and more for garnishing
2 cups cherry tomatoes, and more for garnishing	1 tablespoon avocado oil
1 cup Onion Broth (page 88)	
¼ teaspoon black pepper	

1. Preheat oven to 350°F.

2. Bake the Shortcrust dough in a 10-inch tart pan for approximately 10 minutes, until dry but not too golden. Remove from the oven and let cool.

3. Melt the Homemade Butter in a sauté pan over medium heat. Add the onion slices and cook, stirring often, for 10 minutes to caramelize. Reduce the temperature to low, cover, and let sit for 30 minutes.

4. Add the garlic, basil, maple syrup, balsamic vinegar, and salt. Cook for about 10 more minutes, stirring lightly, until onions are soft, dark, and sweet.

5. Use an immersion blender to blend the caramelized onions into a thick, smooth paste, about 1 minute.

6. In a blender, combine the beans, cherry tomatoes, Onion Broth, black pepper, salt, and crushed rosemary and blend until creamy.

7. Heat the avocado oil in a saucepan. Add the bean mixture and caramelized onions, stirring well. Cooking to heat through, and until the mixture looks thick and dry, about 5 to 6 minutes.

8. Pour the mixture into the cooled Shortcrust, and bake at 350°F for 15 to 20 minutes, or until a thin dry crust forms on the tart.

9. Garnish with fresh rosemary and more cherry tomatoes.

PRO TIP: . . . .
The thinner the onions are sliced, the faster they caramelize.

Chorizo and Asada Taco Bowl

YIELD VARIABLE

Taco bowls are the perfect picnic food, but the best taco bowls need a lot of prepping love to simplify assembly. This recipe allows you to feed any number of people, with layers of fresh and cooked foods that can be served at room temperature, cold, or hot. Use any or all of the ingredients listed below, and don't be afraid to load in anything else your heart desires. The taco bowl is the perfect vehicle for a more is more approach and creative improvisation.

Tortilla Bowl (page 123)	Salsa Fresca (page 102)
	Guacamole (page 102)
1 head lettuce, shredded	Squash Cheese (page 111)
Jackfruit Chorizo (page 98)	Sour Cream (page 82)
	Rice Cheese (page 112)
Mushroom Asada (page 97)	

1. Layer all ingredients into a tortilla bowl in the order listed above, omitting or doubling up as desired.

2. Serve with additional fixings on the side.

PRO TIP: · · · · · · · · · · · · · · · · · · ·
Once ingredients hit the tortilla, there's a time limit to the moisture resilience of the bowl. Make all components ahead and assemble at most 30 minutes before you intend to eat.

Flame-Grilled Stuffed Poblano Peppers

MAKES 6 PEPPERS (SERVES 3 TO 4)

Stuffed peppers are a great way to enjoy flavor and crunch, and layering sauces makes this a festive and colorful dish that packs protein into a quick meal. I prefer the poblanos a little crisp, rather than soft, blackening them just enough to taste a hint of char while maintaining the spicy, toothsome bite of the pepper.

2 cups raw long-grain white rice, and additional cooked rice for serving	6 poblano peppers
2 cups Basic Broth (page 88) (optional)	2 tablespoons Sour Cream (page 82), and more for garnishing
1 tablespoon olive oil	1 tablespoon Squash Cheese (page 111), and more for serving
½ teaspoon cumin seeds	4 cups Feta (page 110) or Ricotta (page 110)
¼ teaspoon salt	

1. Combine the raw rice in a saucepan with 4 cups water, or 2 cups water and 2 cups Basic Broth, the olive oil, cumin seeds, and salt. Bring to a boil, then lower the heat and simmer, covered, for 15 minutes, until the rice is moist and water is fully absorbed. Let stand 5 minutes, then fluff with a fork.

2. Find the flat side of each pepper and cut a flat plane off the opposite side to open the pepper. Remove the seeds (see Pro Tip).

3. Place the peppers open side down on a baking sheet and broil on high for 2 to 3 minutes to lightly blister their outsides without softening the flesh. Remove from the oven.

4. Mix the Sour Cream and Squash Cheese into the Feta, then stuff the mixture into the peppers.

5. Return the peppers to the broiler and broil for 3 minutes, or until the peppers are charred in a desirable pattern. Keep a close eye on them to prevent over-charring.

6. Dress with more Squash Cheese and Sour Cream, and serve with rice slathered in warm Squash Cheese.

Leave the stems on the peppers for easy handling and an attractive appearance, and for an added spicy kick, reserve their seeds and mix them into the filling. The stems help to keep the peppers strong as they roast, and may blacken quicker in the broiler, adding to the smoky aroma.

Ahi Tuna Steak with Wasabi Coconut Peas

In this plant-based version of an ahi tuna dish, sugars from the watermelon form a glaze that comingles with pepper as the steak sears in the pan. A very hot griddle surface, lightly greased, will ensure an even sear that stays intact. The steaks don't need much time to sear. If you prefer a firmer steak, cook for less time. A longer sear will result in a softer steak with more sweetness from the caramelization.

Tuna Steaks

1 small red watermelon	1 tablespoon tamari or Soy-Less Sauce (page 77)
1 small yellow watermelon	1 teaspoon flaxseed oil
Fishy Marinade (page 86), 2 recipe portions	1 teaspoon fresh lemon juice

Searing Flour

2 tablespoons gluten-free flour (or chickpea and rice flour in equal parts), or conventional flour	1 tablespoon ground flaxseeds
	1 teaspoon arrowroot powder
	¼ teaspoon ground white pepper

Wasabi Coconut Peas (page 259) for serving

1. Cut each watermelon in half and then into even slices approximately 2 inches wide.

2. Cut rectangles approximately 3 by 4 inches wide (or to your preference) from the center of each slice. Remove the seeds, but be careful to keep the rectangles in one piece. Save the excess watermelon for Watermelon Gazpacho (page 213).

3. Press the steaks in a clean dishrag under a heavy book or salt block for 3 to 5 minutes.

4. Combine the Fishy Marinade, tamari, flaxseed oil, and lemon juice and mix well. Add the watermelon steaks and marinate in the mixture for 30 minutes at room temperature, flipping a few times and basting the steaks in the marinade to ensure even and thorough absorption.

5. Pat the steaks dry with a clean dishrag, then place the rag on a plate, set the steaks on top to absorb any leftover moisture, and set aside.

6. Combine all ingredients for the searing four, mixing well.

7. Rub a small amount of the searing flour onto the top and bottom of each steak, allowing any excess to fall off.

8. Heat a dry cast-iron griddle or frying pan over medium heat for 2 minutes, then add the steaks and sear on both sides. Their height will reduce and their juices will release, then the sugars will partially merge with the flour to crust the steaks. Use a turning spatula to carefully flip the steaks to protect the surface of the sear and make sure it doesn't separate from the steak.

9. Cook until the sear is even on both sides and the steaks' centers are warm, approximately 4 minutes on each side. Overcooking may result in steaks that are too tender, although they will still be delicious.

10. Serve the steaks over the Wasabi Coconut Peas.

Wasabi Coconut Peas

2 cups green peas, fresh or thawed from frozen and drained

3 garlic cloves, thinly sliced

One 1-inch ginger root, minced

3 tablespoons Pearl Onion Confit (page 195), chopped

½ cup coconut flour

2 tablespoons coconut oil, melted and cooled to room temperature

1 teaspoon wasabi paste or scant ¼ teaspoon wasabi powder

½ teaspoon salt

½ teaspoon black pepper

1. Sauté peas over medium heat for 4 minutes, and let cool to room temperature. Transfer to a bowl and combine with the garlic, ginger, and Pearl Onion Confit.

2. In a separate bowl, combine the coconut flour, coconut oil, wasabi paste, salt, and black pepper and whisk to fully combine.

3. Add the pea mixture to the coconut oil mixture, and toss together to mix thoroughly.

4. Spoon the peas into a plating form, such as a circle, and refrigerate for 10 minutes before removing the form and serving with the watermelon steak.

PRO TIP:

Dust both sides of the finished steaks with a bit more of the searing flour and spice mixture before serving for a pop of flavor at the first bite.

Paella

MAKES 8 TO 10 SERVINGS

Paella is a cornucopia of aromatics and satisfying bites. It needs time and adequate moisture to develop its coveted crust—the socarrat—on the bottom of the rice. It may be tempting to stir the paella, but let it sit—only adding more moisture if the dish dries out before the rice cooks. Although we've photographed this paella in a cast-iron pan, traditionally it is made in a paella pan, which is typically very thin and holds onto less heat than a cast-iron pan. Cooking with a cast-iron pan requires double the broth, as the pan carries a constant high heat and will quickly dry the rice out without the extra fluids. The benefits of this are that extra broth can provide extra flavor, and a higher heat means the potential for a thicker socarrat.

Infused Broth

2 cups Onion Broth (page 88)	¼ teaspoon crushed rosemary
½ red bell pepper, including seeds, finely diced (reserve remaining half for Paella, page 262)	1 teaspoon saffron
	1 cup white wine

Paella

5 tablespoons extra-virgin olive oil

3 to 4 long king oyster mushrooms, stems cut into ½-inch-thick discs

8 ounces haricots verts (green beans)

2 ounces dried porcini mushrooms, rehydrated and drained

2 poblano peppers, slivered

½ red bell pepper, thinly sliced

1 cup Onion Broth (page 88)

1 red onion, thinly sliced

6 garlic cloves, minced

1 sprig rosemary

1 tablespoon smoked paprika

4 Roma tomatoes, diced

3 cups arborio rice, rinsed

Squeeze fresh lime juice

Pinch saffron

8 ounces hearts of palm, sliced into discs

14 ounces marinated artichoke hearts

Capers, to taste

¼ bunch fresh parsley

¼ bunch cilantro (or 1 cup fresh sorrel)

Salt, to taste

Black pepper, to taste

Squeeze of fresh lemon or lime juice

1. Combine the Onion Broth, diced red pepper and seeds, crushed rosemary, and ½ teaspoon of the saffron in a saucepan over medium heat. Bring to a low boil, cover, and reduce to a simmer for 15 minutes. Remove from the heat, uncover, and let stand for 5 minutes.

2. Add the white wine and stir thoroughly. Allow to cool to room temperature, then add the remaining ½ teaspoon of saffron. Set aside.

3. Heat 1 tablespoon of the olive oil in a paella pan over medium-high, add the king oyster mushrooms, and cook for 6 minutes to sear on all sides, then remove and set aside.

4. Add another tablespoon of olive oil to the pan, add the haricots verts, and sear for 4 to 5 minutes until sear marks form along the length of the ingredients. Remove and set aside.

5. Add another tablespoon of olive oil and the porcini mushrooms, poblano peppers, and red pepper slices. Sauté for 5 minutes, until the peppers are tender but not soft, and then set aside.

6. Add ¼ cup of the Onion Broth to the same pan and cook until the liquid almost disappears.

7. In order, add the red onion, garlic, whole rosemary sprig, and smoked paprika. Cook until the onions darken in color, about 6 minutes.

8. Add the tomatoes and the remaining ¾ cup Onion Broth and stir until bubbling.

9. Add the arborio rice and wait 3 to 5 minutes, then add the saffron-infused broth, 1 more tablespoon of olive oil, and the mushroom-pepper sauté. Stir thoroughly one last time and cook until rice is firm but tender, about 18 minutes.

10. Add the oyster mushrooms, a squeeze of lime juice, and the pinch of saffron. Stir gently and cook for 10 minutes, or until a crust forms.

11. Remove from the heat and dress with the haricots verts, hearts of palm, artichoke hearts, capers, parsley, cilantro, a sprinkle of salt, black pepper cracked on top, a squeeze of lemon or lime juice, and the remaining tablespoon of olive oil.

PRO TIP: ·
Allowing the infused broth to sit overnight helps to develop its deep flavors. You can either strain out the solids before using or keep them to simplify the process.

Charcuterie

In a gastropub, a charcuterie board is a requisite menu item, and typically one that is not all that laborious for the kitchen to prepare. Rather, it is a sampling of artisan wares procured from quality vendors. For the vegan chef, it can be a magnum opus of from-scratch kitchen methods, including smokes, bakes, and more. The plate and sauces are every bit as important as the main attractions, and a large variation of textures, colors, and flavors is the key to a phenomenal charcuterie board. On page 266 you'll find a large list of options. Make sure to incorporate a bit from each category, opting for larger portions or more variety depending on the party size. You don't have to make all of these items in one go; you can use just a few, and even use them with other dishes. Mix and match the accompaniments, scaling up for a larger party or a full meal, alternating between sweet and salty, and offering at least one bread choice.

Meaty Components

CHOOSE 3 OR 4

Eggplant Sausage (page 106)

Beet and Radish
Carpaccio (page 268)

Smoked Carrots (page 181)

Shiitake Bacon (page 267)

Sweet Contrasts

USE AS MANY AS DESIRED

Jams and Preserves (page 80)

Candied Citrus Peels (page 300)

Savory Spreads

CHOOSE 1 OR 2

Classic Pesto (page 83)

Tapenade (page 108)

Pâté-Stuffed
Mushrooms (page 191)

Crunchy Additions

CHOOSE 2

Seed Crackers (page 143)

Kale Chips (page 204)

Spiced Blanched
Almonds (page 268)

Creamy Cheeses

CHOOSE AT LEAST 2

Cashew Cream Cheese (page 117)

Brie (page 114)

Ricotta (page 110)

Cauliflower Ricotta (page 111)

Herbed Cashew Cheese (page 116)

Charcuterie Accompaniments

Dates

Castelvetrano olives

Black Garlic (page 107)

Sun-dried tomatoes

Figs

Cherry tomatoes

Pearl Onion Confit (page 195)

Fresh herbs for garnishing

Sourdough bread or
    toasted baguette

Paratha (page 132)

Shiitake Bacon

1 ounce dried shiitake mushrooms, 4 ounces rehydrated

3 cups Porky Marinade (page 87)

1 tablespoon avocado oil or safflower oil

1. Combine the shiitake mushrooms and Porky Marinade in a sealed container and refrigerate overnight to marinate and rehydrate the mushrooms.

2. Preheat oven to 350°F.

3. Separate the rehydrated mushrooms from the marinade; reserve the marinade if also preparing Beet and Radish Carpaccio (page 268). Slice the mushrooms approximately ¼-inch-thick, about 4 to 6 slices per mushroom depending on size.

4. Toss the mushrooms in the avocado oil and spread in an even layer on a baking sheet lined with parchment paper.

5. Bake for 30 to 40 minutes or until the desired crispiness is achieved, flipping every 10 minutes. Keep an eye on the mushrooms to avoid overcooking.

Beet and Radish Carpaccio

MAKES ABOUT 40 SLICES OF CARPACCIO,
DEPENDING ON THE SIZE OF THE ROOTS

3 cups Porky Marinade
(page 87 or reserved from
Shiitake Bacon, page 267)

1 watermelon radish, scrubbed

1 beet, scrubbed

1. Heat the Porky Marinade in a saucepan over medium-low heat, until hot but not close to bubbling. Remove from the heat.

2. Using a mandoline, thinly slice the watermelon radish and beet. Rinse the slices in cold water several times, then add to the warm marinade and marinate for 45 minutes at room temperature.

3. Drain the slices, and roll and skewer, 3 or 4 together or individually, before serving.

Spiced Blanched Almonds

MAKES 2 CUPS

2 tablespoons avocado oil

½ teaspoon crushed rosemary, whole leaved fresh

½ teaspoon oregano, whole leaves fresh

¼ teaspoon tarragon, whole leaves fresh

2 cups whole raw almonds

1 teaspoon smoked paprika

1 teaspoon garlic powder

½ teaspoon salt

½ teaspoon black pepper

1. Combine the avocado oil with the rosemary, oregano, and tarragon and let sit at room temperature to infuse overnight.

2. Preheat oven to 350°F.

3. Working with 1 cup at a time, spread the almonds on the bottom of a wide bowl.

4. Boil 3 cups water and pour just enough of the actively boiling water over the almonds to cover. Let stand for 60 seconds, then immediately drain the almonds and run under cold water. Towel dry.

5. Using your hands, squeeze the skin off of each almond, or use the towel to vigorously remove the skin, one at a time. Repeat with the remaining almonds.

6. Combine the infused oil with the paprika, garlic powder, salt, and pepper and toss the almonds to coat thoroughly.

7. Spread onto a baking sheet lined with parchment paper and bake for 20 to 30 minutes, stirring once. You'll know they're done when the smell hits you and the almonds seem lightly golden and no longer shiny from the oil.

PRO TIP: •
A little goes a long way. Save a small portion of each component from other preparations and assemble later into this plate, or halve the recipes for each component. Your guests will want to save room to try everything they see.

Maitake Steak

MAKES 4 STEAKS

Hen of the woods, also known as maitake, is a complex mushroom with many small lips and a natural tendency to crumble. Pressing the mushrooms condenses their flavors and squeezes out the water, allowing them to soak up a marinade while firming their texture. Playing with the naturally meaty taste and texture of this mushroom, this steak preparation will leave a smoky, savory aroma in the air and a bold impression on the palate. The real gem of this steak is the Maillard reaction, a chemical reaction that occurs at high heat where the juices and proteins create a savory glaze-like effect on the food. That reaction creates aromas, flavors, and textures that will deliver a savory, seared-steak mouthfeel.

Beefy Marinade (omit the salt if using salt blocks) (page 86), 2 recipe portions

Porky Marinade (omit the salt if using salt blocks) (page 87), 2 recipe portions

2 maitake mushrooms

1. Mix the marinades together, and whisk vigorously to combine.

2. Halve the mushrooms through their stems to create 4 flat, broad pieces.

3. Press the mushroom pieces between 2 salt blocks and let sit at room temperature for 45 minutes.

4. Preheat oven to 375°F.

OPPOSITE: Maitake Steak and Fava Bean Tapas with Ibérico-Style Mousse (page 189)

5. Place the pressed mushrooms in a clean bowl and pour the marinade mixture over the top. Allow the mixture to seep into all the nooks and crannies of the mushrooms. Delicately flip the mushrooms in the sauce a few times, then let marinate for 20 minutes.

6. Remove the mushrooms from the marinade, reserving the liquid, transfer the mushrooms to a salt block or baking sheet, and weigh down with another salt block or baking sheet.

7. Place the salt block or baking sheet in the oven, with pressure maintained on the mushrooms, and cook for 18 to 20 minutes, flipping once halfway through. A stronger and browner mushroom that is dry at the edges but still moist in the center is the goal.

8. Heat a cast-iron skillet over medium-high heat. Pour some of the reserved marinade mixture into the pan, and finish the mushroom steaks by searing on high until a Maillard reaction occurs on the mushrooms and the sides brown.

9. Serve with the reserved marinade, au jus.

PRO TIP: ·
Serving on a hot salt block or a lava stone is an excellent visual touch, and will keep the steaks warm.

Seitan Piccata

The Seitan Scaloppini at New York City's Blossom restaurant was a major revelation to me when I was wrestling with my renewed veganism after an intermission as a dedicated gourmet foodie. One bite confirmed that being vegan didn't mean making an ascetic choice to forsake all delicious food, and certainly didn't mean that I would be doomed to eat only blended kale shakes for the rest of my life. Years later, I was inspired to develop my own scaloppini, a chicken-style piccata, in homage to Blossom and so I could continue to enjoy it as I ventured away from New York. I have paraded it in front of many skeptical omnivore friends and family members over the years to show the possibilities of vegan cuisine, and it has worked. Maybe this piccata will open doors for you, or for stubborn relatives, like Blossom's scaloppini did for me.

1 pound Seitan Chicken (page 95), thin and flat (¼ inch, sliced or made to measure)

¼ cup all-purpose flour

2 tablespoons arrowroot powder

1 teaspoon salt

1 teaspoon black pepper

1 ¼ teaspoons fresh thyme

Neutral cooking oil (safflower oil, sunflower oil, or avocado oil)

1 white onion, thinly sliced

3 garlic cloves, thinly sliced

Zest of ½ lemon (approximately ½ tablespoon)

Peel of ½ lemon, in thin strips, with additional peel strips reserved for garnishing

Juice of 1 lemon (approximately 1 ½ tablespoons)

10 green olives (such as Picholine or Cerignola), pitted and sliced

¼ cup finely chopped parsley

2 tablespoons finely chopped cilantro

⅔ cup dry white wine

2 cups Basic Broth (page 88)

1 ½ ounces capers with brine, and more for garnishing

2 tablespoons nutritional yeast

1. Coat the Seitan Chicken in a mixture of the flour, arrowroot powder, salt, black pepper, and ¼ teaspoon of the thyme, and set aside on a baking sheet lined with parchment paper.

2. Heat the safflower oil in a sauté pan over medium heat, add the onion and garlic, and sauté until softened, about 4 minutes. Add strips of lemon peel. Cook until the onions turn transparent, then add the olives, half of the parsley, and half of the cilantro.

3. Add the white wine and bring to a rolling boil.

4. Add the Basic Broth and the remaining thyme, cilantro, and parsley, and reduce to simmer for 10 minutes.

5. Add the lemon juice, capers, and nutritional yeast, and simmer 2 to 4 minutes more.

6. Add the cutlets, two at a time, and cook until browned on both sides, approximately 6 minutes per side.

7. To serve, sprinkle fresh lemon zest on top, and garnish with strips of lemon peel and extra capers, if you love them as much as I do.

PRO TIP: •
A slightly underworked seitan dough produces a good height and isn't too chewy. I usually make fatter cutlets, and then fillet in half to the desired thickness, rather than overworking the dough into a thin, broad piece.

Lasagna Skyscrapers

MAKES 8 TO 10 SKYSCRAPERS TO SERVE 3 TO 4 PEOPLE

Take your zucchini lasagna one step further by diversifying the ingredients with the rest of a late-summer bounty. Layering different hearty vegetables, some grilled and some roasted, imparts savory and sweet flavors. Height always plays well on the plate, and photographs even better. These skyscrapers are bound together by rich sauces, their stacks are deceptively filling, and they look refined and elegant without too much effort.

Vegetable Discs

1 teaspoon sugar	1 skinny butternut or crookneck squash, peeled and cut into ⅓-inch discs
½ teaspoon salt	
½ teaspoon dry rosemary, crushed	1 skinny sweet potato, peeled and cut into ⅓-inch discs
½ teaspoon dry marjoram	
¼ cup sunflower oil	1 medium-width zucchini, cut into ⅓-inch discs
	1 heirloom green tomato, cut into ⅓-inch discs

1. Preheat oven to 350°F.

2. Mix the sugar, salt, rosemary, and marjoram, with the sunflower oil.

3. Toss the squash and sweet potato discs in the oil mixture.

4. Transfer the discs to a baking sheet, reserving the remaining oil, and roast the vegetables for 20 minutes. Flip and brush with more of the oil mixture, then roast for another 12 to 15 minutes, until tender enough to cut with a butter knife. Set aside. These can be prepared up to 3 days prior to assembly and serving.

5. Baste the zucchini and tomato discs with the remaining herbed oil mixture. Heat a cast-iron grill pan over medium heat, add the zucchini, and cook for approximately 3 minutes. Flip the zucchini, add the tomato to the pan, and cook until the zucchini is golden on both sides and the tomato is tender, approximately 3 minutes more.

Fire-Roasted Broccoli Rabe

1 bunch broccoli rabe	Sprinkle salt
Neutral cooking oil (such as safflower oil, sunflower oil, or avocado oil)	Squeeze fresh lemon juice for garnishing

1. Using a spray bottle, lightly spray the broccoli rabe with the cooking oil, being careful not to saturate it, then sprinkle with salt.

2. With tongs, hold the broccoli rabe over the flame of the stove and rotate it until some of its edges blacken, about 30 seconds per side.

3. Before serving, dress with a squeeze of lemon juice.

Sun-Dried Tomato Sauce

1 cup sun-dried tomatoes	½ teaspoon garlic powder
½ cup fresh basil	Salt and pepper, to taste
¼ cup fresh oregano	¼ cup olive oil
2 tablespoons nutritional yeast	1 tablespoon fresh lemon juice (about ½ lemon)

1. Rehydrate the sun-dried tomatoes by placing in warm water and letting them soak for at least 2 hours. Remove the tomatoes and set the soaking liquid aside.

2. Combine the tomatoes and all the remaining ingredients in a blender or food processor. Add 2 tablespoons or more of the reserved soaking liquid and pulse until a very rough paste is formed.

3. The sauce can be made up to 1 week in advance, and kept in a jar with a tight-fitting lid in the refrigerator until ready to use.

Arugula Basil Pesto

1 cup fresh basil	½ teaspoon garlic powder
1 cup arugula	Pinch salt, or more to taste
1 tablespoon Cashew Cream Cheese (page 117) or Cauliflower Ricotta (page 111)	½ cup olive oil
	1 tablespoon fresh lemon juice (about ½ lemon)

1. Combine all ingredients in a blender or food processor and blend until a smooth paste is formed. The pesto can be made up to 1 week in advance, and kept in a jar with a tight-fitting lid in the refrigerator until ready to use.

Assembly

1 cup Cashew Cream Cheese (page 117) or Cauliflower Ricotta (page 111)	Olive oil for garnishing
	Nutritional yeast for garnishing
¼ cup pine nuts, roasted or lightly toasted	Arugula for garnishing

1. Starting with either the squash or sweet potato, cut each with a round mold to make it the perfect size and then shape to match the diameter of the zucchini and tomato. Stack the vegetables alternating just one of each in any one stack, and ending with the tomato. Layer the veggies with one each of the sauces in between, approximately 1 teaspoon of sauce per layer. Use more sauce to make a messy lasagna, or less for a clean look.

2. End with the tomato on top and a dollop of either Cashew Cream Cheese or Cauliflower Ricotta.

3. Top with pine nuts, a drizzle of olive oil, and a sprinkle of nutritional yeast.

4. Garnish the plate with more pine nuts and a bed of arugula with the Broccoli Rabe running the length of the sides of the dish. If a more polished look is preferred, drizzle the arugula with oil before adding the broccoli.

PRO TIP: ·

Picking ingredients with similar diameters is really important, but there is a lot of flexibility in presentation. For example if only very thick zucchini is available, you could try slicing them on the broad side using a mandoline so the zucchini forms a flat layer, like a lasagna noodle, to build up layers of your stacks, or sandwich in between flat zucchini.

Polenta Tian

This ratatouille-inspired tian is layered with herbed polenta and hearty vegetables in a quick homemade tomato sauce. Sounds like a little plate of heaven to me. I like to stack the ingredients vertically to form a stripe for an active visual rhythm, but a flat layered scheme, more like a lasagna—see page 224, middle left—works just as well.

Zucchini and Tomato Marinade

3 tablespoons tamari or Soy-Less Sauce (page 77)	2 small zucchinis or ½ large zucchini, thinly sliced
1 tablespoon sesame oil	4 large Roma tomatoes, the same diameter as the zucchini, thinly sliced
1 teaspoon smoked paprika	

Eggplant Marinade

2 tablespoons flaxseed oil	1 large Japanese eggplant, the same diameter as the zucchini and tomatoes, thinly sliced
1 teaspoon red wine vinegar	
1 teaspoon sesame chili oil (or if heat isn't desired, use toasted sesame oil)	

Sauce

5 large tomatoes	1 teaspoon garlic powder
½ white onion	½ teaspoon rubbed sage
2 garlic cloves, chopped	Salt, to taste
1 cup Basic Broth (page 88) or a tomato-based broth	2 ½ to 3 pounds Polenta from Scratch (page 109), formed into tubes and sliced into discs
½ cup fresh basil, and more for garnishing	Nutritional yeast, to taste
2 tablespoons fresh oregano	

1. Combine the tamari, sesame oil, and paprika in a bowl. Add the zucchini and marinate for at least 30 minutes.

2. Remove the zucchini, place in a covered container, and set aside. Add the tomatoes to the zucchini marinade and marinate for at least 30 minutes.

3. Combine the flaxseed oil, red wine vinegar, and sesame chili oil in another bowl. Add the eggplant and marinate for at least 30 minutes.

4. Meanwhile, start cooking the sauce. Combine the tomatoes, white onion, garlic, and Basic Broth in a cast-iron pan on medium heat. Cook down the vegetables for 45 minutes, adding the basil and oregano toward the end of the cooking time. Transfer to a container to cool. If desired, this can be made up to 3 days in advance of usage and kept in the refrigerator; make sure, however, to allow it to return to room temperature before use.

5. While the sauce cooks down, heat a large sauté pan over medium-high heat. Add the zucchini and sear for 3 minutes each side, then remove from the pan and set aside. Add the eggplant to the same pan and sear for about 3 minutes each side, then set aside with the zucchini.

6. Combine the garlic powder, sage, and salt, and rub the polenta discs with the mixture. Place the polenta in the same pan you used to cook the vegetables and sear until lightly crispy on both sides.

7. Preheat oven to 400°F.

8. Assemble the tian in a large round baking dish that's not too deep. Add the sauce to the bottom of the pan, and begin alternating discs of zucchini, eggplant, tomato and polenta, always making sure to overlap the vegetables if assembling the flat style, otherwise packing tightly on their side for the vertical style. Finish with a final layer of sauce, reserving some sauce for the end of the bake.

9. Bake the layered tian for 30 minutes, dressing with more sauce toward the end.

10. Sprinkle fresh basil and nutritional yeast over the tian after removing it from the oven. Serve hot, but let stand at least 10 minutes before trying to cut into it.

PRO TIP: ·
Nothing beats homemade tomato sauce, especially in a simple rustic dish like this, but store-bought or made-ahead works fine. I often find homemade tomato sauce tastes better after a resting day.

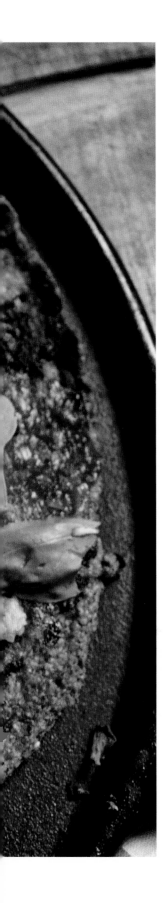

Polenta Pissaladière

MAKES 8 SLICES, OR 4 SERVINGS

If you want to jam as much flavor onto a crust as possible, this is the flatbread for you. Pissaladière, a rustic French take on pizza, is a main attraction—not a side dish. And it will make you wonder if the French or the Italians do it better. (Pizza making, I mean.) The aromatic crust and onion sauce draw inspiration from Mediterranean and French cuisine. Feel free to improvise the toppings—it's still a pizza, after all.

Caramelized Onions

2 tablespoons Homemade Butter (page 79)	2 sprigs fresh thyme, leaves only
4 medium sweet onions, finely diced	1 tablespoon maple syrup
2 garlic cloves, minced	1 teaspoon white balsamic vinegar
¼ cup fresh basil	5 drops black seed oil
	½ teaspoon salt

Crust

2 tablespoons ground flaxseeds	1 teaspoon celery seeds
1 cup medium coarse cornmeal, and more for sprinkling	1 teaspoon crushed red pepper
½ cup gluten-free flour	1 teaspoon salt
¼ cup nutritional yeast	½ teaspoon black pepper
1 teaspoon baking powder	⅔ cup melted Homemade Butter (page 79)
1 tablespoon cumin seeds	Neutral cooking oil (safflower oil, sunflower oil, or avocado oil)
1 teaspoon dried basil	
1 teaspoon dried oregano	
1 teaspoon dried rosemary	

Toppings

Black olives, ideally in salt brine, not oil

Capers in rock salt

Shiitake strips tossed in dulse flakes

Cashew Cream Cheese (page 117) or Cauliflower Ricotta (page 111)

Cherry tomatoes

Fresh basil

Fennel fronds

1. To caramelize the onions, heat a sauté pan over medium heat, add the Homemade Butter and the onions, and cook for 10 minutes, stirring well, then reduce the heat to low, cover, and cook for 30 minutes.

2. After 30 minutes, add the garlic, basil, thyme, maple syrup, white balsamic vinegar, black seed oil, and ½ teaspoon salt. Stir to combine and cook uncovered for 10 more minutes, or until the onions are soft, dark, and sweet.

3. While the onions caramelize, make 2 flax eggs by mixing the ground flaxseeds with 5 tablespoons warm water. Let sit.

4. Use an immersion blender to blend the caramelized onions into a thick but smooth paste. Set aside.

5. Preheat oven to 350°F.

6. In a medium bowl, combine the cornmeal, flour, nutritional yeast, baking powder, basil, oregano, rosemary, cumin seeds, celery seeds, crushed red pepper, salt, and black pepper and stir to mix.

7. Add 3 cups water, the flax eggs, and the melted Homemade Butter to the dry ingredients. Work the mixture thoroughly with your hands, wetting your palms lightly if necessary to prevent the dough from sticking to your hands.

8. Coat a cast-iron pizza or crepe pan in neutral cooking oil, then heat on the stovetop for 2 minutes on medium heat.

9. Once the oil is hot, turn off the flame, and sprinkle a thin layer of the cornmeal in the pan before adding your batter. Spoon in the batter and spread it to cover the pan evenly and completely.

10. Transfer to the oven and bake for 15 minutes, or until the crust is dry at the center. Remove from the oven and add the caramelized onion sauce and all the other toppings.

11. Return to the oven for 8 to 10 minutes, or until the toppings are slightly brown and soft and the bottom of the crust lifts easily and is dark around the edges.

PRO TIP: ·
This crisps perfectly in a cast-iron crepe pan or on a pizza stone; the former makes a very attractive serving dish.

Cauliflower Steak en Croute

MAKES 2 SERVINGS

Cauliflower, one of the most versatile vegetables, is filling and gives a satisfying bite. Tender but hearty, this "en croute" version makes a knife-and-fork meal, with a striking appearance all on its own. Complete the dish with a seasonal side like a Chef's Salad (page 202) or sautéed greens.

Marinade

½ cup Beefy Marinade (page 86)

1 teaspoon cumin powder

¼ teaspoon ground fennel seeds

¼ teaspoon cinnamon powder

¼ cup fresh cilantro

¼ cup tamari or Soy-Less Sauce (page 77)

2 tablespoons olive oil

Two 1 ½-inch-thick slices of cauliflower

Crust

3 tablespoons tapioca starch

2 tablespoons coarsely ground walnuts

2 tablespoons coarsely ground pecans

2 tablespoons coconut shreds

2 tablespoons ground flaxseeds

2 teaspoons coriander powder

1 teaspoon coffee grounds

¼ teaspoon black pepper

¼ teaspoon salt

1. Preheat oven to 400°F.

2. Combine all the marinade ingredients in a gallon-sized zip-top bag, then add the cauliflower and seal. Let sit for 30 minutes at room temperature, flipping occasionally.

3. Mix all the crust ingredients together thoroughly in a large bowl.

4. Remove the cauliflower from the marinade and coat generously with the crust mixture, allowing it to fill the cracks in the cauliflower. Place the coated cauliflower on a parchment-lined baking sheet.

5. Bake for 15 to 20 minutes, flipping once halfway through, or until a dry crust has formed on the cauliflower.

Squid Ink Two Ways

This delicious and surprising sauce goes very well with either black rice or black bean pasta to enhance the intended "squid ink" color. The marriage of umami and sweet flavors and the seaweed blend is an unusual combination that reveals more of itself the more you eat it.

½ cup walnuts

12 dried shiitake mushrooms

10 pieces dried porcini mushrooms

14 ounces uncooked black bean pasta or 2 cups uncooked black forbidden rice

½ teaspoon whole cumin seeds

Flaxseed oil, 1 ½ teaspoons if using pasta or ½ teaspoon if using rice

¼ teaspoon sea salt, if using pasta

2 tofu skin sheets (usually in rolls of 4-by-10 inches when unrolled)

¼ cup tamari or Soy-Less Sauce (page 77)

2 tablespoons seaweed powder blend (mix of 1 tablespoon dry wakame, 1 sheet nori, crumbled, 1 teaspoon dulse powder, ¼ teaspoon green spirulina, and ¼ teaspoon chlorella)

3 tablespoons black bean aquafaba

2 tablespoons miso paste

1 tablespoon blackstrap molasses

1 teaspoon toasted black sesame oil

2 large garlic cloves

1 tablespoon onion powder

2 teaspoons kala namak (Indian black salt)

½ teaspoon shiitake powder

½ teaspoon mushroom powder (porcini, maitake, or bolete)

Baby greens for garnishing (optional)

White sesame seeds for garnishing (optional)

1. Lightly toast the walnuts in a dry pan for 6 minutes. Combine the walnuts, shiitake mushrooms, and porcini mushrooms with 3 cups warm water and set aside to soak for 30 minutes.

2. Cook the black bean pasta or black forbidden rice according to the package directions, with the cumin seeds. If using pasta, rinse under cool water and then toss in 1 teaspoon flaxseed oil and the sea salt. Set the cooked pasta or rice aside.

3. Drain the walnuts and mushrooms, reserving the liquid.

4. Cut the tofu skin sheets into ring shapes, like calamari. Combine the ½ teaspoon flaxseed oil, 2 tablespoons of the tamari, 1 tablespoon of the seaweed powder blend, and half of the liquid from the soaked walnuts and mushrooms in a bowl, and add the tofu skin rings. Marinate for 20 minutes at room temperature.

5. Heat a sauté pan over medium heat and add the tofu skin rings, discarding their marinade. Sauté until lightly golden and crisp at the edges, about 8 to 10 minutes.

6. In a blender, combine the remaining half of the liquid from the walnuts and mushrooms with the black bean aquafaba, miso paste, blackstrap molasses, toasted black sesame oil, garlic, onion powder, kala namak, shiitake powder, mushroom powder, the remaining 2 tablespoons tamari, and the remaining 1 tablespoon seaweed powder and blend until it reaches a very smooth and creamy consistency.

7. Slice the soaked mushrooms.

8. Toss the pasta or rice in the blended sauce mixture, then toss in half of the sliced mushrooms, three-quarters of the soaked walnuts, and the tofu-skin calamari.

9. Top with the rest of the sliced mushrooms and walnuts, and garnish with baby greens and white sesame seeds.

PRO TIP: ·
Pacaya palm seasoned with Fishy Marinade (page 86) makes a great substitution for the tofu skin sheets in this dish. When sautéed rather than battered and fried, the textured palm will resemble squid.

Palak Paneer

Traditional Indian foods are natural choices for vegetarians and can easily be made vegan with a few substitutions. With some love, tofu can mimic paneer, an uncured cheese common in India. In India, using tofu is becoming so popular that tofu is often labeled "soy paneer." The trick to a great Palak paneer is to combine two textures of seasoned spinach: one blended into the sauce, and one sautéed for a chewy texture that keeps the mouth interested while treasure-hunting for the soy paneer. Serve with wild rice cooked with cumin seeds and Homemade Butter (page 79), and add Paratha (page 132) on the side for a complete Indian meal.

Blended Spinach Sauce

1 pound spinach	2 teaspoons ground sea salt
1 cup full-fat coconut milk (canned)	1 ½ teaspoons Garam Masala (page 31)
4 garlic cloves	1 teaspoon cumin powder
One 1-inch ginger root, peeled and chopped	1 teaspoon cardamom powder
2 tablespoons nutritional yeast	

Soy Paneer

¼ cup avocado oil	1 teaspoon salt, and more, to taste, for finishing
¼ cup fresh fenugreek leaves (optional; if you can't find fresh, ideally use ¼ teaspoon fenugreek powder)	1 teaspoon cumin powder
	½ teaspoon garlic powder
1 teaspoon cumin seeds	½ teaspoon Garam Masala (page 31)
1 teaspoon black mustard seeds	8 ounces baby bella mushrooms (optional)
10 ounces firm tofu, pressed, drained, and cubed	2 green cardamom pods, cracked
1 tablespoon nutritional yeast	1 pound shredded spinach

1. Combine all ingredients for the blended spinach sauce together in a blender and pulse until the spinach leaves are broken down.

2. Heat 2 tablespoons of the avocado oil in a tall-walled sauté pan over medium heat and add the fenugreek leaves, cumin seeds, and black mustard seeds. Cook, stirring often, until the fenugreek leaves are completely wilted, about 6 minutes. (If using powdered fenugreek instead, do not use yet.) If not using fresh leaves, just dry toast the seeds for 2 minutes until aromatic.

3. Toss the cubed tofu with the remaining 2 tablespoons avocado oil in a bowl. Add the nutritional yeast, salt, ground cumin, garlic powder, and Garam Masala, and toss to coat thoroughly.

4. Add the coated tofu to the sauté pan and panfry until it is golden and the texture becomes crispy and crunchy around the edges.

5. Add the baby bella mushrooms to the pan, if using, and cook for 2 to 3 minutes. Add the blended spinach sauce, stir, and add the green cardamom pods. If using powdered fenugreek, add it now.

6. Add the shredded spinach and cover for 2 minutes to fully wilt.

7. Stir completely, taste, and add salt and garlic to taste.

PRO TIP: ·
Look for broad leaf spinach. This recipe can be made with baby spinach, but nothing beats a hearty whole leaf spinach for this savory mix. Also, you'll need more spinach than you think, so stick to the listed weight (2 pounds total).

DESSERTS

OPPOSITE: Plum Trio Galette (page 305)

Life is uncertain,
eat dessert first.

—

Ernestine Ulmer

DESSERT ELEMENTS

Cashew Sweet Cream

MAKES APPROXIMATELY 2 CUPS

- 2 cups cashews, soaked and then drained
- ⅓ cup full-fat coconut cream (canned)
- ⅓ cup maple syrup
- 2 tablespoons fresh lemon juice (about 1 lemon)
- 1 tablespoon Madagascar vanilla extract
- Pinch Himalayan salt

1. Combine all ingredients in a blender and blend until smooth.

2. Store in a jar with a tight-fitting lid and refrigerate. Keeps for up to 2 weeks. Also works well stored in a squeeze bottle to be used for decorating desserts.

Coconut Whipped Cream

MAKES APPROXIMATELY 1 ½ CUPS

- 1 ¾ cups full-fat coconut cream (canned), refrigerated overnight
- ¼ cup powdered sugar
- 1 teaspoon arrowroot powder
- 1 teaspoon vanilla extract

1. In a chilled bowl, combine all ingredients and whisk by hand to combine.

2. Transfer the mixture to a chilled whipped cream charger, if available. Chill between uses, and discard after 2 days.

3. If a whipped cream charger is not available, pour the whisked mixture into a freezer-safe bag and freeze for 20 minutes, then remove from the freezer and crush and integrate by hand.

4. If using a shaped tip, place mixture in a pastry bag with the tip attached. Otherwise, snip off a corner of the freezer bag to use as a makeshift piping bag.

5. Store in the refrigerator, but freeze for 10 minutes prior to using and agitate bag to loosen just before topping. Use immediately for best results, but keeps for up to 3 days.

Candied Citrus Peels

MAKES 2 CUPS

2 cups citrus peels, cut into strips with pith intact but no fruit attached

1 ½ cups organic sugar, and more to coat

Food coloring or natural food coloring, such as blue or green spirulina, butterfly pea powder, pitaya powder, safflower powder, or turmeric powder (optional)

1. Combine the citrus peels and 4 cups cold water in a bowl. Let sit for 15 minutes, then drain well.

2. Transfer the peels to a small saucepan, cover with water, and boil for 15 minutes.

3. Drain the peels, return them to the saucepan and re-cover with water, and return to a boil for another 15 minutes. Then drain again, re-cover with water once more, and boil for another 10 minutes. If peels are light in color and tender (as more delicate peels like lime should be), move on to the next step. If not, simmer on medium-low heat for 15 to 25 minutes until they become tender.

4. Drain the peels and set aside.

5. Combine the sugar and 1 ½ cups water in the saucepan and heat over medium heat to make a simple syrup. Once the sugar dissolves, add the food coloring, if using.

6. Bring the syrup to a minimum temperature of 210°F, but no higher than 225°F. This will take approximately 25 minutes.

7. Add the peels to the mixture and boil in the syrup for 5 minutes, then reduce heat and simmer for 15 minutes.

8. Remove the peels carefully from the syrup, and let excess liquid drip over a wire rack and into the saucepan.

9. Transfer the peels to a baking sheet lined with parchment paper. After 2 to 3 minutes, as the syrup begins to set, sprinkle the peels with sugar, taking care to coat them evenly.

10. Store at room temperature in an airtight container lined with parchment paper. For optimum flavor, eat within 3 months.

Candied Edible Flowers

MAKES 12 CANDIED FLOWERS

1 dozen medium-sized edible flowers (such as nasturtiums, violas, borage, or squash blossoms)	1 tablespoon caster sugar or finely ground sugar
	Food coloring (optional)
¼ cup cornstarch	1 drop flavoring extract, such as vanilla or almond (optional)

1. Pat the flowers with a paper towel, very gently brushing to remove any moisture on the petals. Keep the stems intact to help hold the flowers while dipping.

2. Mix the cornstarch, caster sugar, and food coloring and flavoring, if using, with 1 tablespoon water to create a thick slurry.

3. Dip the flowers in the slurry one at a time.

4. Set the flowers on parchment paper and paint one at a time with the slurry. Paint the back side first and then flip the flower over, smooth the front side flat, and paint it too.

5. Let the flowers dry on a wire drying rack with plenty of airflow. Use immediately once dry.

PRO TIP: ·
Candied flowers and citrus peels make a beautiful decoration for Tarts (page 321) and other pastries such as Crème Brûlée (page 335). They are delicious on buttered Scones (page 129), atop salads, and even as a garnish for a cocktail.

DESSERTS

Crème Patisserie

MAKES JUST UNDER 1 QUART

12 ounces silken tofu, drained

¾ cup Plant Milk (Oat Milk, page 356, or Almond Milk, page 33, works best)

¾ cup agave

⅓ cup coconut oil

2 ¼ tablespoons Madagascar vanilla extract

6 tablespoons coconut flour

1 ½ teaspoons tapioca starch

1. Combine the tofu, Plant Milk, agave, coconut oil, and vanilla extract in a blender and blend on low to combine.

2. Whisk the coconut flour and tapioca starch together in a small mixing bowl.

3. Pour the blended mixture into a saucepan over medium heat and add the flour and starch mixture, stirring constantly to thicken.

4. When the mixture comes to a light bubble, stir vigorously and then remove from the heat. Continue to stir a few times after removing.

5. Return the mixture to the blender and pulse until smooth.

6. Allow to cool before piping or adding to tarts. Best if used within 2 days, but keeps in the fridge for up to 1 week.

PRO TIP: •
For flair, add food coloring or flavoring during the final blend.

Marshmallows

1 ½ cups powdered sugar

½ cup liquid sweetener (like maple syrup)

¾ cup aquafaba, at room temperature

1 teaspoon xanthan gum

2 teaspoons vanilla extract

Cornstarch or powdered sugar to coat (optional)

1. Combine the powdered sugar, liquid sweetener, and ½ cup warm water in a saucepan over medium heat and heat until the mixture reaches 240°F to 250°F, checking often with a candy thermometer.

2. Remove the saucepan from the heat and cover to keep warm.

3. Whip the aquafaba and xanthan gum together in a stand mixer with the whisk attachment until the mixture becomes stiff and foamy.

4. While whipping, slowly pour a thin stream of the sugar syrup into the aquafaba and xanthan gum mixture, over the span of 1 minute. When the candy is fully combined and the mixture forms strong, stiff peaks, add the vanilla extract and whip to combine.

5. Transfer the mixture to a rimmed baking tray (ideally ½ to ¾-inch-deep) or a greased mold and refrigerate for at least 3 to 4 hours, until marshmallows spring up after a light fingertip press.

6. Cut into the desired shapes and sift cornstarch, if using, over the marshmallows to coat.

7. Store in a zip-top bag at room temperature. Keeps for up to 1 month.

Plum Trio Galette

A fresh fruit galette is one of the most charming pastries. Galettes are relatively fast and easy to make, gorgeous, and can spotlight almost any fruit combination. This galette is warm and inviting, adaptable to the seasons, and definitely photo-worthy with its smooth, shiny finish. It also has a delightfully strong crust, allowing the pieces to be picked up with ease—a perfect treat for a party or to share with kids. Because galettes have an open window framed by crust, they are the perfect vehicle to add color and design to an otherwise rustic country bake. By selecting multiple color variations of the same fruit, like this galette, which has three colors of plum (golden, purple, and red), you can alternate for rhythm or cluster for bold color designs.

Crust Dough

1 ½ cups all-purpose flour

1 tablespoon coconut flour

Large pinch sea salt

2 tablespoons ground flaxseeds

¼ cup coconut oil, kept cold while working

1 tablespoon maple syrup

1. Combine the all-purpose flour, coconut flour, and sea salt in a glass bowl and chill in the fridge for 10 minutes.

2. While the above chills, make 2 flax eggs by mixing the ground flaxseeds with 5 tablespoons water. Let sit until all ingredients are chilled and ready for step 3.

3. Remove the dry ingredients from the fridge. Using a pastry cutter, slowly combine the flax eggs, cold coconut oil, and maple syrup with the dry ingredients.

4. Slowly add ½ cup ice water, 1 tablespoon at a time, and use the pastry cutter to mix.

5. On a lightly floured piece of parchment paper placed on a chilled marble board or baking sheet, roll out the dough to ¼ inch thick.

6. Transfer the parchment-lined marble board or baking sheet to the fridge to chill the dough for 1 hour.

Frangipane

2	cups almond meal	1	tablespoon maple syrup
2	tablespoons Spring Preserves (page 81) or any store-bought sweet jam	¼	teaspoon cardamom powder
		¼	teaspoon cinnamon powder
2	tablespoons Cashew Sweet Cream (page 299)	¼	teaspoon vanilla bean powder
1	tablespoon cordial or sweet liqueur (like amaretto)		Pinch nutmeg powder

1. While the dough for the crust is chilling, combine all ingredients for the frangipane filling in a bowl and mix with a fork until fully incorporated. Set aside until ready to assemble the galette.

Glaze

¼	cup Spring Preserves (page 81), blended smooth	1	tablespoon water, sweet wine, or fruit liqueur
2	tablespoons maple syrup		

1. Combine all ingredients in a small saucepan over medium heat and whisk to combine.

2. Heat until completely liquefied, whisking occasionally.

3. Strain if necessary, then return to the saucepan and heat over a very low flame to keep warm (not hot) until ready to assemble the galette.

Fruit and Assembly

	7 to 9 plums, depending on size (use golden, purple, and red)	1	teaspoon orange zest
		1	teaspoon tapioca starch
1	tablespoon fine organic cane sugar		Sprinkle demerara sugar
½	teaspoon lemon zest	2	ounces crystallized ginger, finely diced, for topping

1. Slice plums, and wrap in a towel to reduce excess liquid.

2. Preheat oven to 350°F.

3. Remove the crust dough from the fridge and trim the edges to create whatever shape you prefer: round is standard, but not required. A shaped rolling cutter can also be used to create fun shapes.

4. Transfer the shaped dough to a room temperature baking sheet freshly lined with parchment paper.

5. Cover the dough with frangipane filling, stopping 1 inch from the edges. Smooth the filling evenly.

6. Toss the plum slices in the cane sugar, zest, and tapioca, then arrange over the crust, alternating colors and pressing them into the frangipane. Leave no space between the fruit slices. Load up on the fruit if desired, but do not expand beyond the frangipane.

7. Fold over the edges of the crust, pinching and pressing the folds.

8. Brush the fruit and pastry with the glaze.

9. Bake, covered with foil, for 40 minutes.

10. Uncover, brush the crust with more glaze, and then sprinkle with demerara sugar. Check the bottom of the pastry to see if the crust is crisp or soft. When ready, it should have a hard and smooth surface, but still have some give to it to ensure that it will be delicate and moist. If it's not ready, rotate the baking sheet and continue baking for up to 10 to 15 minutes more. (If you are baking on the lowest rack in the oven, the bottom will crisp more quickly, so less time may be needed.)

11. When fully baked, remove the galette from the oven. While still hot, paint the pastry with more syrup and top with crystalized ginger crumbles. Add more demerara sugar if desired.

PRO TIP: ·
You can also use a fruit jelly to glaze the crust instead of the syrup glaze. Ginger jelly or marmalade would be particularly tasty paired with this recipe.

Triple Layer Cheesecake

Bright and colorful, layered raw cheesecakes are as dazzling to the eye as they are to the taste buds. The filling for this cheesecake, enriched by sweet cashew meat and coconut milk, offers a luscious, creamy texture that outshines that of a conventional cheesecake. Fruit toppings are optional, as is the crust. Just make sure the cake completely sets before you remove it from the pan.

Crust

1 cup almond flour	¼ cup coconut oil
1 cup dates (9 or 10 dates)	½ teaspoon vanilla extract
¾ cup shredded coconut	½ teaspoon cinnamon powder
½ cup walnuts	¼ teaspoon salt
½ cup cashews	Pinch clove powder
½ cup ground flaxseeds	

Filling

5 cups cashews, soaked overnight and then drained	3 tablespoons fresh lemon juice (about 1 ½ lemons)
1 ¼ cups full-fat coconut milk (canned)	2 tablespoons vanilla extract
½ cup maple syrup	1 teaspoon nutritional yeast
½ cup coconut oil	½ teaspoon salt
¼ cup kombucha	

Layers

½ cup freeze-dried blueberries

¼ cup frozen blueberries

1 teaspoon blue spirulina (optional)

½ cup freeze-dried raspberries

½ cup frozen cherries

¼ cup freeze-dried cherries or freeze-dried strawberries

1 teaspoon beet root powder

1. Line the base of a 6-inch springform pan with plastic wrap or a bakery round, or lightly grease the bottom and sides of the pan.

2. Combine all the crust ingredients in a food processor and mix until they form a dense ball. Press the crust mixture into a flat, even disc at the base of the springform pan. Freeze for at least 20 minutes.

3. Combine all the filling ingredients in a blender and blend until smooth, then divide the filling into 3 equal portions.

4. Return 1 portion of the filling to the blender, add the freeze-dried and frozen blueberries, and blend until smooth. This will make the first layer of the cake. If you'd like to marble the top of the cake, measure out one-quarter of the blueberry layer, add 1 teaspoon blue spirulina to it, and set aside. Pour the remaining blueberry mixture (or all of it, if not marbling the top layer), into the pan on top of the frozen crust. Make sure it settles smooth, flat, and even, tapping gently to release any air bubbles. Freeze for 30 to 45 minutes.

5. Clean out the blender, return the second portion of filling to the blender, add the freeze-dried raspberries, and blend to make the second layer. Pour on top of the frozen first layer, making sure it settles smooth, flat, and even, tapping gently to release any air bubbles. Freeze for 30 to 45 minutes.

6. Clean out the blender and return the third portion of the filling to the blender. Add the frozen cherries, freeze-dried cherries, and beet root powder and blend. If marbling the top of the cake, set aside one-quarter of the third portion before blending with the fruit and beet to keep it white; pour the rest on top of the second layer and make sure it settles smooth, flat, and even, tapping gently to release any air bubbles.

7. To marble the top, after spreading the red layer smoothly across the set second layer, dollop spoonfuls of the two reserved batches on top of the third layer, alternating colors. Use the handle of the spoon or a chopstick to swirl them together and create a marbled effect.

8. Freeze the layers together for at least 2 hours, or ideally overnight. Transfer to the fridge to thaw for 1 to 2 hours before serving.

PRO TIP: •
While the second and third portions are waiting to be used, they should sit at room temperature so they don't firm up. Also, do not skip the freeze times between layers. If left to fully freeze overnight once fully assembled, the cheesecake will keep well in the fridge.

Pumpkin Bread

MAKES 12 SERVINGS

Quick breads are a delicious accompaniment to any meal, and pumpkin bread was required at all my family gatherings for the fall holidays, especially Thanksgiving. I always use my largest vintage Bundt pan to make quick breads. It's 10 ¼ inches across and holds 10 cups—and even with this massive bake, the bread never lasts very long. The bread tastes best when made with fresh pumpkin (I always save the pumpkin guts from my jack-o'-lanterns to keep a healthy supply on hand) or squash puree, which will provide the right flavor and can be easier to find year-round. Serve this bread as is or sprinkled with powdered sugar at breakfast, or even as a seasonal dinner side.

3 cups all-purpose flour	1 teaspoon salt
1 cup plus 3 tablespoons brown sugar	1 ½ cups pumpkin or squash puree
½ cup white sugar	½ cup applesauce sauce, or another ½ cup pumpkin puree plus 1 tablespoon maple syrup
1 ¾ teaspoons baking soda	
1 ½ teaspoons cinnamon powder	1 ½ cups full-fat coconut milk (canned)
1 teaspoon nutmeg powder	¾ cup sunflower oil

1. Preheat oven to 375°F, and grease a Bundt pan with a neutral cooking oil such as safflower oil, using a towel to spread the oil evenly into every crevice.

2. In a large mixing bowl, sift together the flour, sugars, baking soda, cinnamon, nutmeg, and salt.

3. In a separate mixing bowl, combine the pumpkin, applesauce, coconut milk, and sunflower oil.

4. Mix the wet ingredients slowly into the dry ingredients, using a whisk or the paddle attachment on a stand mixer on low-medium speed until fully incorporated.

5. Transfer the mixture to the prepared Bundt pan.

6. Bake for 30 minutes, then reduce the temperature to 345°F and bake another 30 to 40 minutes.

7. Use a toothpick to test for doneness; the bread is done when the toothpick comes out clean. If it is not ready, continue baking, but be careful not to overbake.

8. Allow the pumpkin bread to cool to room temperature on a cooling rack before attempting to remove it from the pan, but begin to free its edges with a toothpick or knife while it is still warm. After cooling, use a knife to completely free the pumpkin bread from the pan before inverting.

PRO TIP: ●

This bread can easily be made gluten-free by using a standard gluten-free flour. For a gluten-free version, reduce the heat to 350°F for the entire bake and allow the toothpick to come out a little dirty before removing. An underbake is usually better for gluten-free bakes, where moisture is usually the deciding factor for deliciousness. For banana bread, replace the pumpkin puree with 1 ½ cups mashed bananas (approximately 4 or 5 ripe bananas), and consider adding ¾ cup of chocolate chips.

Sous Vide–Tempered Chocolate

6 OUNCES TEMPERED CHOCOLATE, ENOUGH TO MAKE 24 TO 30 MOLDED CHOCOLATES

Sous vide is the perfect method for tempering chocolate. The sous vide machine makes it possible to control the temperature of your chocolate, easily the most critical part of chocolate making. By protecting your hand with a heatproof kitchen glove, you can agitate the mixture in the water to help the crystals align for a chocolate that shines once set, whether using seed chocolate to encourage your crystal alignment or going completely from scratch. Tempered chocolate can be used to make the Peanut Butter Cups on page 319, to decorate the tops of cakes or puddings, to make molded truffles, as a dip for fruit, and more.

2 cups vegan melting chocolate discs
(or two 3-ounce vegan chocolate bars)

Tempered Chocolate

1. Break or cut the chocolate into fine pieces. The smaller the better, but not so small that the chocolate melts or becomes a powdery mess.

2. Seal the chocolate in a sous vide pouch, either with a pump or with a zip top, using the water immersion method (page 317). Weighing the bag with a clip-on weight will be helpful, but I don't recommend using in-bag weights.

3. Set the water temperature to 115°F. Using a heatproof glove, lift the bag to check the temperature (infrared works best) and to knead the chocolate, getting as much circulation as possible. Keep the bag itself as close to 113°F as possible for 3 to 5 minutes while kneading to ensure even distribution.

4. Set the water temperature to 81°F and remove water 1 cup at a time, replacing it with ice to speed up the cooling process.

5. Knead the chocolate.

6. When the sous vide reaches 81°F, count 20 seconds and then immediately set the temperature to 90°F.

7. Keep kneading the chocolate. When you are ready to use it, simply snip a corner of the bag and pipe it into molds, onto fruit, or onto a chilled board to set chocolate designs.

Water Immersion Method (For Sealing Bags in a Sous Vide)

1. Fill a zip-top bag three-quarters full, leaving one-quarter of the space empty. (Make sure to use a bag the appropriate size for the volume of ingredients inside, and note that when using this method, a zip-top bag with a slide is much easier.)

2. Fill a sous vide container (preferably a 12- to 24-quart graduated, flat-walled, dry/wet food-grade container) with water. Slide or zip the bag so that air can only escape from a very small opening, and manually press out as much air as you can.

3. Slowly lower the bag into the water, ¼ inch at a time, allowing the water to displace the air in the bag and the bag to collapse in on itself. Do this until you reach the top, and then angle the bag so the slight opening is the last bit to reach the water surface line.

4. As the small opening reaches the surface line, squeeze the bag to compress any remaining air pockets, and ensure that the bag is flat. It will look vacuumed tight. Carefully close the remaining opening while lowering, being very careful to ensure no water enters the bag. When you remove the bag from the water, it should retain its vacuumed appearance.

PRO TIP: •
Tempered chocolate is a labor of love. You will still have well-shaped and delicious chocolate if you pour melted chocolate into a mold while skipping the steps above. But remember, never add water or liquid ingredients to chocolate at any time.

Shaped Chocolate

1. Pipe tempered chocolate into any shape mold (chocolate molds, caramel molds, and ice cube molds work best). To make truffles, pipe the chocolate into a spherical mold (I love a domed flower shape as well).

2. Chill in the fridge so the chocolate sets quickly. The quicker you cool the chocolate, the better it will set. The sign of a properly tempered chocolate is that it will come to a glossy shine at room temperature.

Chocolate from Scratch

3 tablespoons cocoa butter	1 cup cocoa powder
1 cup caster sugar or fine sugar	

1. Melt the cocoa butter in a double boiler.

2. Cream the sugar into the cocoa butter with a silicone spatula, keeping in the double boiler, until no grit remains.

3. Add the cocoa powder slowly, stirring with the spatula. Keep stirring until fully integrated, with no lumps or oil separation.

4. Heat over medium-low heat to exactly 90°F.

5. As soon as it reaches 90°F, pour into a bar mold and place in the fridge.

6. Follow the instructions on page 315 to temper.

7. Add any desired add-in. Some add-ins, such as sea salt, can be placed into the liquid chocolate after poured into a mold for aesthetic effect or stronger contact with the tongue.

Suggested Additions for Chocolate (But Use Anything That Sounds Appealing!)

Soy milk powder or coconut milk powder	Chili powder
Demerara sugar	Sea salt
Vanilla bean powder	Freeze-dried blueberries
	Candied ginger

Sous Vide–Tempered Chocolate Peanut Butter Cups

MAKES APPROXIMATELY 30 PEANUT BUTTER CUPS
IF USING A STANDARD SIZE CUPCAKE TIN AS A MOLD

Sous Vide–Tempered Chocolate, 2 recipe portions

PEANUT BUTTER FILLING (PICK ONE):

1 cup creamy peanut butter, ¼ cup organic caster sugar or organic powdered sugar, and 2 tablespoons melted Homemade Butter (page 79), mixed until fully incorporated and chilled until ready to use

OR

1 ½ cups peanut butter, preferably crunchy and salted

OR

1 cup creamy or chunky peanut butter and 3 tablespoons agave or ¼ cup maple syrup, mixed until fully incorporated and chilled until ready to use.

1. Line any size cupcake pan—from mini to Texas muffin-sized—with cupcake liners.

2. In each liner, layer the tempered chocolate, then the desired peanut butter mixture, then more tempered chocolate. Make sure the peanut butter mixture stays in the middle and the chocolate goes around the peanut butter enough to coat the sides of the liner to form a wall.

3. Tempered chocolate will set at room temperature, but to speed along the process, you can put the assembled cups in the fridge and they should set in about an hour. Store at room temperature in a food storage container with a lid, or if your kitchen is very warm, you can store in the fridge in the same container.

Fruit Tarts

There's nothing more attractive than a fresh fruit tart, colorful and enticing loaded up with every fruit you can find fresh at the market. With these tarts, your kitchen counter will look like a French patisserie in no time. Feel free to add additional fruits or candied flowers, and keep then on display under a cake dome for all to see. The lemon curd has a gorgeous yellow appearance that complements flowers like violets and deeper colored toppings like figs, whereas the coconut matcha tart has a bright green color, a great contrast to strawberries or shredded coconut, but be creative.

Lemon Curd Fruit Tarts

MAKES ENOUGH FOR 3 TARTLETS

1 cup silken tofu (about ¾ of a 16-ounce package)	¼ teaspoon turmeric powder
½ cup fresh lemon juice (3 or 4 large lemons)	2 drops lemon extract
½ cup agave	1 ½ tablespoons arrowroot powder or tapioca starch
¼ cup avocado oil or safflower oil	1 ½ teaspoons agar crystals
1 ¼ tablespoons fresh lemon zest (zest of about 1 large lemon)	Shortcrust (page 138), ¾ recipe portion, or Coconut Tart Crust (page 140), 1 recipe portion (optional)

1. Combine the tofu, lemon juice, agave, avocado oil, lemon zest, turmeric powder, and lemon extract in a blender and blend until smooth.

2. Transfer to a saucepan over medium heat and cook, whisking often, for 3 minutes.

3. Mix the arrowroot powder and agar crystals in a small bowl, add 2 tablespoons water, and stir to combine. The mixture will form a thick but even paste.

4. Bring the filling ingredients in the saucepan to a light bubble, reduce the heat to low, and add the arrowroot-agar paste. Heat for 3 to 5 minutes, stirring often, or cook a little longer over a higher heat for a firmer tart filling.

5. Return the mixture to the blender immediately after heating and pulse 2 to 3 times.

6. Let cool for 3 to 5 minutes at room temperature, then transfer to tart crusts or ramekins and refrigerate for at least 1 to 2 hours to set.

Coconut Matcha Fruit Tarts

MAKES ENOUGH FOR 3 TARTLETS

1 can full-fat coconut milk (approximately 13 ounces), refrigerated overnight	2 tablespoons arrowroot powder or tapioca starch
⅓ cup agave	1 teaspoon agar crystals
1 teaspoon hazelnut or vanilla extract	2 tablespoons coconut water
4 teaspoons matcha powder (bright green ceremonial grade is best)	Shortcrust (page 138), ¾ recipe portion, or Coconut Tart Crust (page 140), 1 recipe portion (optional)

1. Combine the coconut milk, agave, hazelnut or vanilla extract, and matcha powder in a blender and blend until smooth.

2. Transfer to a saucepan over medium heat and cook, whisking often for 3 minutes.

3. Mix the arrowroot powder and agar crystals in a small bowl. Add the coconut water and stir to combine. The mixture will form a thick but even paste.

4. Bring the filling ingredients in the saucepan to a light bubble, then reduce the heat to low and add the paste. Heat for 3 to 5 minutes, stirring often, or cook a little longer over higher heat for a firmer tart filling.

5. Return the mixture to the blender immediately after heating and pulse 2 to 3 times.

6. Let cool for 3 to 5 minutes at room temperature, then transfer the filling to a tart crust or ramekins and refrigerate for at least 1 to 2 hours to set.

Chocolate Mousse Tarts

There are very few occasions that are not made better with a little chocolate. This velvety and smooth chocolate mousse is a decadent dessert that provides an opportunity to flex your piping skills. Use a ribbon tip for a clean and modern pleated look, or a star tip to make rosettes, or get creative with a design of your own. The dark chocolate color and flavor is well complemented by tart toppings such as raspberry, which can be incorporated into your design with enhanced mouthwatering effects.

2 ½ cups chocolate chips (16 ounces)

1 package silken tofu (16 ounces)

⅓ cup Plant Milk (page 33)

3 tablespoons agave

2 teaspoons vanilla extract

Fresh fruit for garnishing (optional)

Shredded coconut for garnishing (optional)

Colorful sugar for garnishing (optional)

Maldon salt for garnishing (optional)

Shortcrust (page 138), 1 ½ recipe portions, or Coconut Tart Crust (page 140), 2 recipe portions (optional)

1. Melt the chocolate chips in a double boiler or bain-marie.

2. Combine the melted chocolate, tofu, Plant Milk, agave, and vanilla extract in a high-speed blender and pulse until smooth.

3. Transfer the mixture to a glass mixing bowl and chill in the fridge for 1 hour.

4. Pipe or spoon chocolate mousse into a tart crust or ramekins.

5. Garnish and decorate as desired with fresh fruit, shredded coconut, or colorful sugar.

6. Chill in the refrigerator for at least 4 hours to set before serving.

PRO TIP: •
Use the three types of fillings on pages 321 to 323 to create an infinite number of flavor combinations. You can also layer all three of the fillings in one tart or use the Crème Patisserie (page 302) as a filling or to pipe on top.

Key Lime Berries and Cream

MAKES 2 TO 4 RAMEKIN-SIZED SERVINGS

This deconstructed crustless tart with zesty lime cream surrounding fresh berries is a simplified twist on a traditional comfort classic. The presentation largely depends on the vessel, as it can be made to look formal or informal, even playful. It can also be served as individual skewered crème-filled berries (crème-filled berry kebabs). See the photo of it on page 118.

6 tablespoons fresh lime juice

Crème Patisserie (page 302), 1 recipe portion

5 large strawberries per small ramekin (about 20 strawberries total)

5 large raspberries per small ramekin (about 20 strawberries total)

1 tablespoon lime zest for garnishing

Candied lime peel for garnishing

1. Combine the lime juice and Crème Patisserie and stir to mix.

2. Coat the bottom of each of two large or four small ramekins with the lime Crème Patisserie, then refrigerate for 2 hours to set. Spoon the unused Crème Patisserie into a piping bag with a star tip and refrigerate.

3. Cut the bottom points and greens off the strawberries and use a wide icing tip to core them.

4. Remove the ramekins from the fridge and arrange the strawberries and raspberries in the crème with the wide parts facing up.

5. Using the piping bag, swirl crème into the hollow of each berry.

6. Garnish each serving with lime zest and candied lime peel.

PRO TIP: •

Load all the berries into the serving dish before piping in the cream, so they stay in place. Served as "berry kabobs," these make a fun summer treat, and can be arranged on a platter in different linear shapes, like stars.

Minty Rocky Road Ice Cream

Rocky road ice cream does not disappoint the texture lovers among us. Crunchy and sweet, chewy with a touch of dark chocolate bitterness, it hits every note. The image shows the bricks to the rocky road formed in mini-muffin pans, but the ice cream can also be swirled into a tub like conventional ice cream and scooped out. This recipe has a minty twist which I prefer for rich chocolate and nuts, but if classic rocky road flavors are preferred, use a plain simple syrup instead.

Mint Syrup

½ cup fresh mint leaves

1. Boil 1 cup water; add the mint.

2. Reduce the heat to low and heat for 3 to 5 minutes.

3. Drain to remove the solids.

Mint Simple Syrup

½ cup organic sugar   ½ cup brewed mint tea

1. Combine the sugar and mint tea in a saucepan on medium heat and simmer, stirring often, for 5 minutes, until the sugar dissolves.

2. Bring to a light bubble for 5 minutes, then reduce the heat to low for 10 minutes. Cook until the syrup forms balls when drizzled on a cold spoon.

Base

3 frozen bananas	¼ cup maple syrup
½ cup peanut butter	

Chunky Ingredients

¼ cup cacao nibs	10 large Marshmallows, chopped, or 1 cup mini Marshmallows (page 303)
2 tablespoons cacao powder	
¼ pound macadamia nuts, halved	

1. Blend the bananas, peanut butter, and maple syrup in a food processor until creamy, but still firm.

2. Drizzle in either the Mint Syrup or the Mint Simple Syrup 1 tablespoon at a time, to taste. Process to whip until the volume of the base expands.

3. Transfer the mixture to a freezable container lined with enough plastic to wrap the top, then fold in the chunky ingredients.

4. Cover with the plastic wrap and lid and freeze for 2 to 4 hours, or up to 2 weeks. Ice cream may need to thaw before serving or scooping.

> **PRO TIP:** •
> Vegan marshmallows can be challenging to make at home, so you can skip the struggle with these two recommended commercial varieties: Sweet and Sarah, and Dandies. Don't love mint? Substitute simple syrup in place of the mint simple syrup.

Avocado Pistachio Ice Cream

This ice cream is an Instagram-worthy presentation with a healthy twist and will delight your guests, kids, or raw vegan friends. The whimsical avocados combine fruits and nuts and won't leave dishes for you to clean up—just toss them on the compost pile. The best part? The edible pit can be popped out and saved as a treat for later or made on its own and enjoyed as a raw vegan donut hole.

Ice Cream

3 avocados	½ teaspoon pistachio or hazelnut extract
2 frozen bananas	¼ teaspoon green spirulina (optional, for color and health benefits)
⅔ cup full-fat coconut milk (canned)	
⅓ cup agave	

Pits

6 dates, pitted	¼ cup hazelnuts
¼ cup pistachios	¼ cup almond meal

Glaze

¾ cup melted coconut oil, cooled to room temperature	¼ cup powdered sugar
¼ cup cocoa powder	¼ teaspoon cinnamon powder

1. Cut the avocados in half, remove and reserve the pits and flesh, and reserve the shells. Transfer the flesh of 1 whole avocado to a food processor; save the flesh of the remaining 3 avocados for another use.

2. Add the bananas, coconut milk, agave, pistachio extract, and spirulina to the food processor and whip on high speed to encourage frothing.

3. Divide the mixture among the emptied avocado shells and place in bowls to keep level in the freezer. Freeze the ice cream in the avocado shells for 2 to 3 hours.

4. Meanwhile, scrape out the food processor used for the ice cream, but do not clean, and add all ingredients for the pits. Process to chop until the pieces are small and consistent. Do not overprocess.

5. Scrape down the sides of the food processor and transfer the pit mixture to a mixing bowl.

6. Roll balls from the mixture to replicate the size and shape of avocado pits. Place onto a parchment-lined baking sheet and put directly into the freezer. Freeze for 1 to 2 hours.

7. When the ice cream and pits are frozen, whisk all ingredients for the glaze in a bowl with a base about the width of a baseball (avoid using a wider, shallow bowl).

8. Remove the frozen pits from the freezer. Roll and submerge each pit in the glaze mixture.

9. Using a fork or candy tongs, lift the pit out of the glaze, letting any excess drip off, and place the pits on a baking sheet lined with parchment paper. Be careful not to let the glaze pool and set flat at the base of the balls.

10. Remove the avocado shells from the freezer and use the real reserved avocado pits to indent the ice cream, then use an ice cream scooper to hollow out a hole the size and shape of the pits.

11. Place the glazed frozen pits in the hollows in the ice cream, and let the desserts thaw in the fridge for up to 25 minutes, or at room temperature for 5 minutes, before serving.

PRO TIP: •

The extracts are largely interchangeable, so feel free to experiment and choose your own flavor combination, choosing a non-nut flavor if desired. For a thicker glaze on the pit that resembles the glaze on a donut hole, allow the glaze to set and then dip once more. Alternatively, you can increase the cocoa powder in the glaze by 1 to 2 tablespoons.

Flan

Flex your caramel-making muscle with this flan, and decide whether you would like a crackling sugar top or an oozing, sauce-like caramel. These are best made in silicone cupcake molds, and I find the extra-large muffin size to be especially wonderful. Traditional recipes use rum as the flavoring, but you can experiment with different extracts like bergamot or almond. I first created this veganized classic to surprise my dear friend Rachel,* whose dairy allergy prevents her from indulging in her favorite childhood dessert. She cried when I showed up with a tray of flan at her thirtieth birthday, and she ate the better part of that tray in one day.

Custard

1 ½ cans (approximately 19 ½ ounces) full-fat coconut milk	¼ teaspoon kala namak (Indian black salt)
1 can coconut cream (approximately 12 ounces)	¼ teaspoon cardamom powder
12 ounces silken tofu	⅛ teaspoon turmeric powder
⅓ cup sugar	⅛ teaspoon salt
2 tablespoons vanilla extract	¼ cup agar crystals or 1 ½ tablespoons agar powder
1 teaspoon rum extract	1 tablespoon tapioca starch

Caramel

1 ½ cups sugar (if using organic cane sugar or a coarser sugar, add ¼ cup water to help dissolve)	¼ cup agave or corn syrup

---

*   Rachel tells me that her abuela's secret was to use sweet vermouth instead of rum.

1. Combine all the custard ingredients except the agar and tapioca starch in a blender and blend until smooth.

2. Transfer to a large saucepan over medium-high heat and bring to a light boil.

3. While the custard heats, grease a 12-cup cupcake pan, and set aside.

4. In a small saucepan, heat the sugar and agave over medium-low heat to melt and create caramel and reach an internal temperature of 275°F (check with a candy thermometer). Next divide the caramel evenly among the wells to cover the bottom of each one, and swirl to combine. Keep the caramel lined cupcake tins close to the stove to stay warm and pliable while completing step 5. If you want a little more working time, keep a dish about as wide as your cupcake tin filled with hot water and place the cupcake tin on top of this bain-marie to stay warm and soft while you work.

5. Stir the agar and tapioca into the custard and boil for exactly 5 minutes, then return the mixture to the blender and blend until smooth.

6. Spoon the custard into the cupcake pan, before the caramel sets too firm (or keep warm as described above).

7. Remove from the heat and chill for 4 to 6 hours in fridge or 1 hour in the freezer. Refrigerate until 30 minutes before serving.

PRO TIP: •

The hotter the caramel temperature, the harder the crack. You can always melt down the caramel with a bit of water if you want to try again. Not used to working with sugar that sets very fast? Float the silicone mold on a hot pan of water to give you a bit more working time and encourage the custard to fuse with the caramel.

Crème Brûlée

Crème brûlée is one of those rare treats that most people only have the opportunity to enjoy at fine dining spots. Even rarer are the vegan versions. Don't be intimidated by the glossy sugar crust and the luscious interior. Get your creative juices flowing with some exotic flavor inspiration and you will soon realize why your home kitchen is better than any restaurant. Amélie made everyone focus on the satisfaction of cracking of the sugar top with a spoon—a texture that is made possible with a blowtorch. But using a blowtorch is a pretty satisfying experience itself, in my personal opinion, and as Julia Child says, "every woman should have a blowtorch." I agree, Julia, I agree.

White Chocolate Bergamot

- ¾ cup full-fat coconut milk (canned)
- ⅓ cup agave or liquid cane sugar
- 3 tablespoons melted cocoa butter
- 1 ½ tablespoons tapioca starch
- ½ teaspoon bergamot extract
- Pinch salt
- Caster sugar or fine white sugar for topping

Violet Macadamia

- 1 cup macadamia nuts, soaked and then drained
- ½ cup full-fat coconut milk (canned)
- ⅓ cup agave
- 2 teaspoons violet extract
- 2 tablespoons tapioca starch
- Pinch salt
- Caster sugar or fine white sugar for topping

Pistachio Rose

1 cup pistachios, soaked and then drained

½ avocado

½ cup maple syrup

¼ cup full-fat coconut milk (canned)

2 tablespoons rose water

2 tablespoons tapioca starch

Caster sugar or fine white sugar for topping

For Each Version:

1. Combine all ingredients except the caster sugar in a blender and blend until smooth.

2. Transfer to a saucepan over medium heat and bring to a very light bubble for 5 minutes.

3. Divide the mixture between two 4-inch ramekins and let cool at room temperature to set. Usually, the crèmes brûlées do not need baking, but if moisture or humidity is keeping them from setting, finish with a light bake. For a firmly set crème, bake at 325°F for 10 minutes.

4. Sprinkle the tops with an even layer of caster sugar and lightly torch until the color starts to change, making several quick back-and-forth passes over the surface.

PRO TIP: ·
The sugar on top should melt and fuse into what resembles a pane of glass.

COCKTAILS AND OTHER BEVERAGES

OPPOSITE: Sangria (page 345)

A cocktail can be made by the bartender. But the cocktail also can be made by the chef.

—

José Andrés

FROM THE BAR

Libertine Old-Fashioned

MAKES 1 SERVING

The return of the classic cocktail to menus was such a welcome sight for me slinging juice in bars of Lower East Side restaurants. These classic cocktails become the blueprints to build on top of for some fun crafted variations. A French and American combination, using rye with Grand Poppy reminiscent of an old-fashioned or a vieux carré (with Grand Poppy in place of non-vegan bénédictine), this care-free cocktail is for classic cocktail lovers who don't want to veer too far, and don't want to miss out either.

Fine sugar for rim

1 ounce cognac

1 ounce rye whiskey

1 teaspoon Cointreau

1 teaspoon Grand Poppy or other vegan sweet American amaro

Sparkling water (approximately 3 to 4 ounces) for topping

Lemon peel for garnishing (optional)

Orange slice for garnishing (optional)

1. Pour the sugar into the bottom of a shallow bowl. Lightly wet the rim of a short tumbler, and dip it into the bowl to coat the rim. Set aside.

2. In a mixing glass, combine the cognac, rye, Cointreau, and Bénédictine. Add ice and stir. Pour the mixture, including the ice, into the tumbler.

3. Top with sparkling water, and garnish with a piece of lemon peel or an orange slice, if desired.

Tropicana Freeze

This frozen daiquiri is the best of both worlds with tequila and rum swirling together, but for a more classic feel, feel free to select the spirit you prefer and match the volume. Tropical fruits in a frozen drink are a natural combination: the bold passion fruit, bright citrus, and colorful raspberries add a sour sharpness that balances the spirits and is lifted by the sugar and the salted rim. Passion fruit is by far my favorite tropical beverage flavor, and while this recipe calls for fresh, you can substitute for 1 tablespoon of passion fruit syrup or ¼ cup passion fruit puree if those are easier to find.

2 ounces tequila	Juice of 1 lime (approximately 1 ½ tablespoons)
2 ounces white rum	2 tablespoons liquid cane sugar
½ cup passion fruit, seeds removed	Coarse salt for rim
½ cup frozen raspberries	Lime wedges for garnishing
Juice of 1 orange (approximately ¼ cup)	Orange slices for garnishing

1. Place two margarita glasses, or one extra-large daiquiri glass, in the freezer to chill.

2. Combine all ingredients except the salt, lime wedges, and orange slices for garnishing in a blender, add 2 cups ice, and blend until smooth.

3. Remove the glasses from the freezer, and wet the rims. Spread the salt out on a plate and place the glasses rim side down into the salt to coat their edges.

4. Fill the glasses, and garnish with lime wedges and orange slices.

Sangria

We all know loosely what a sangria is, but in practice sangria can be a lot of different things, and the type of wine chosen makes all the difference in the world. Complementing many dishes in the book, from the Paella (page 261) to the Ceviche (page 179), sangria need not be saved for Latin dishes, but can be a nice sweet and flavorful accompaniment to bolder-flavored dishes from any region. Perfect for large gatherings that will go on into the night, or afternoons where you can get lost in long conversations among friends, infuse your wine with the flavors of the fruits and herbs of the season, starting with these recipes to spark your creativity.

White

1 peach, diced and bruised	½ cup raspberries, bruised
4 kumquats, quartered	1 bottle pinot grigio
1 Honeycrisp apple, cored and diced	1 tablespoon agave (optional)
1 lime, sliced	Additional fruit for garnishing

Red

1 cup green grapes, gently mashed	1 tablespoon maple syrup (optional)
½ cup strawberries, bruised	2 tablespoons sweet vermouth
1 lemon, sliced	2 tablespoons fresh basil, rolled and bruised
1 bottle rioja	Additional fruit for garnishing

For each version

1. Muddle all the fruits, except those for garnishing, in a large pitcher until the juices are released. Add the wine and sweetener, and if making the red sangria, add the sweet vermouth.

2. Stir to combine until the sweetener is dissolved completely and evenly. If making the red sangria, add the basil.

3. Refrigerate overnight.

4. Serve chilled in wine glasses, and garnished with additional fruit.

The Alchemist

I fell in love with Brennivín the moment I first tried it in Iceland in 2016. Caraway and many other spices and herbs compose the complex flavor of the schnapps, a traditional spirit type for Scandinavia, with the generic name "aquavit" reminiscent of medieval alchemy's aqua vitae as well as the origin of the root word for whiskey. With that kind of lore, I've matched this aquavit spirit with other typically spiritual ingredients from holy basil to Palo Santo and angelica served with a dramatic and sensory smoke float to create an elixir with the power to transform your evening into a golden memory.

- 3 ounces aquavit (Brennivín or other similar)
- 1 teaspoon angelica syrup
- 1 dropper DRAM Palo Santo bitters
- 1 dropper holy basil tincture
- Smoked applewood chips for serving

1. Pour the aquavit into a chilled highball glass and add 1 large round ice cube. Swirl to chill.

2. Add the angelica syrup, bitters, and holy basil tincture and swirl to combine until the syrups aren't visible.

3. Using a handheld smoker pipe with the applewood chips, top with 3 or 4 swirls of smoke.

PRO TIP:

If you can't find aquavit, you may use vodka in its place. Violet syrup or another floral syrup may be used instead of angelica, but angelica and holy basil have health benefits, as well as some connections to alchemy, so they're worth seeking out. These tinctures can be found in most natural food stores and herbalist shops. Gourmet cocktail shops usually stock DRAM and other interesting bitters.

Paris at Sunset

MAKES 1 SERVING

My two favorite cocktails, the corpse reviver and the French 75, combine with a superfood boost from dazzling pitaya (dragon fruit). The absinthe and the elderflower add sweetness and complexity when balanced against each other, and the botanical gin keeps expanding the dimension of flavor on the palette. My favorite part of this cocktail is the layering, creating a sunset of colors almost neon joined by the candied lime peel garnish.

¼ teaspoon pitaya powder

½ ounce gin (a botanical variety like The Botanist or Ransom works well)

½ ounce elderflower liqueur

¼ teaspoon green absinthe

About 4 ounces champagne

Raspberry for garnishing

Candied lime peel for garnishing

1. In order, pour the pitaya powder, gin, elderflower liqueur, and green absinthe into a champagne flute.

2. Gently pour the champagne over the mixture, and allow to settle and reveal the colorful layers.

3. Garnish with a raspberry and candied lime peel.

OPPOSITE: Paris at Sunset and Fava Bean Tapas with Ibérico-Style Mousse (page 189)

Bloody Mary

Outside of your favorite vegan restaurant you aren't likely to find a vegan Mary because of its traditional ingredient: Worcestershire sauce, which typically contains anchovies or a fish sauce. Bottled vegan Worcestershire sauces do exist, but they are hard to find. Making it from scratch can be the best option, and also gives you control over the spice level and savoriness. And building the flavor of the drink is only half the fun; lavish garnishing has become the expected presentation for Bloody Marys. Whether you plan out your garnishes or offer a build-your-own-Mary approach for guests, having a vegan Mary in your repertoire is required in my opinion. After all, is a brunch without a Bloody Mary even a brunch? See the photo of it on page 144.

8 Roma tomatoes

½ cup liquid from Salsa Fresca (page 102)

Juice and zest of ½ lemon (approximately 2 tablespoons juice and 1 teaspoon zest)

Juice and zest of ½ lime (approximately 2 tablespoons juice and 1 teaspoon zest)

1 tablespoon pickle brine or olive brine

½ teaspoon Worcestershire Sauce (page 75)

1 teaspoon grated horseradish (or more if you're wild)

1 teaspoon celery salt

¼ teaspoon black pepper

Hot sauce of choice, to taste (optional)

About 1 cup vodka (1 ½ ounces per serving)

Garnishes: Choose as few or as many as you would like

Smoked Carrots (page 181)

Cherry tomatoes

Celery stalks

Beet and Radish Carpaccio (page 268)

Olives

Shiitake Bacon (page 267)

Jalapeño slices

Shishito peppers

Cracked black pepper

Lemon and lime wedges

Pickles (page 48)

1. Cut an X shape into the top and bottom of each tomato.

2. In a large saucepan, bring 4 quarts of water to a boil, and blanch the tomatoes for 2 minutes.

3. Remove the tomatoes and peel off their skins, starting from the X, where the skin should already be peeling.

4. Allow the tomatoes to cool, and then place in a blender. Add the Salsa Fresca liquid, citrus juice and zest, pickle brine, Worcestershire sauce, horseradish, celery salt, black pepper, and hot sauce, if using, and blend until smooth. Transfer to the fridge to chill for 15 to 25 minutes.

5. To serve, fill a glass with ice, pour in 1 ½ ounces of the vodka, and stir to chill. Fill with the tomato mixture, and leave room for your desired garnishes.

Buttered Brandy

Hot brandy and homemade butter with warming spices are all you need to kiss those winter blues goodbye. Not even cold Boston nights can touch the thermal power of a hot buttered brandy, which is why this American colonial classic cocktail remains a holiday season favorite. This classic can also be made with rum and cider instead of brandy (3 parts cider to 1 part rum), and the seasonal flavors go well with hot beverages regardless of which base you choose.

- 1 cup brandy
- 3 whole cloves
- 1 whole cinnamon stick
- ½ cup melted Homemade Butter (page 79), warm but not hot
- ½ cup demerara sugar
- 1 teaspoon molasses

- 1 teaspoon cinnamon powder
- ½ teaspoon ginger powder
- ¼ teaspoon nutmeg powder
- Zest of 1 small orange
- 1 tablespoon freshly squeezed orange juice
- Coconut Whipped Cream (page 299), for topping

1. Combine the brandy with the cloves and cinnamon stick and let sit to infuse overnight.

2. Cream together the Homemade Butter, demerara sugar, molasses, cinnamon powder, ginger powder, nutmeg powder, and orange zest, in a stand mixer or electric hand mixer on medium, and transfer to a small saucepan over low heat.

3. Add 2 cups hot water to the saucepan, and bring to a light bubble.

4. Remove from the heat and add the orange juice and brandy.

5. Transfer to a hot beverage cup by straining out the solids and filling the cup ¾ full. Top lavishly with Coconut Whipped Cream.

PRO TIP: ·

For a festive presentation, garnish with cinnamon sticks or deep-hued demerara sugar. For a rich, wintery flavor, add 1 drop peppermint extract, ½ teaspoon shaved cocoa butter, and a sprinkle of cacao powder on top.

Irish Cold Brew

MAKES 2 SERVINGS

Don't let the name fool you, Irish Cold Brew can be a hot Irish coffee like no other you have had before. The "cold" in cold brew refers to the initial extraction process, done in a cool temperature over a long period of time, avoiding some acidity and creating the perfect opportunity for more flavor complexity. When served hot, which helps develop that familiar coffee aroma, you might even like it better than brewed coffee. With ingredients like Baileys Almande, an almond milk liqueur, the classic Irish coffee is back for vegans, but Irish creams can be made vegan at home as well, following the instructions below. See the photo of this drink on page 144.

2 cups Cold Brew coffee (page 355)

2 ounces Irish whiskey (like Jameson Black Barrel Reserve or Redbreast 12 year)

2 ounces Baileys Almande, chilled (or ¼ cup Oat Milk (page 356), chilled, blended with 1 tablespoon maple syrup, ½ teaspoon vanilla extract, and ½ teaspoon cinnamon powder)

1 cup Oat Milk (page 356)

Cinnamon or cacao powder for garnishing (optional)

1. If serving cold, combine the Cold Brew, chilled Baileys (or your Irish cream substitute ingredients), and whiskey, and stir to combine, then set aside. If serving hot, transfer the Cold Brew to a small saucepan over medium-low heat and slowly heat to desired temperature, then remove from the heat and add Irish cream and whiskey, then set aside, covered to keep warm.

2. If you have a milk frother, froth the Oat Milk until you achieve a nice, robust foam. If you don't, heat the milk in a saucepan over medium heat, whisking vigorously and constantly until it bubbles and froths. An immersion blender or hand mixer will give you a foamy Oat Milk without heating a cold coffee.

3. Divide the whiskey mixture evenly between two heatproof cups if serving hot, or in a tall glass over ice if serving cold, and then add the foamed Oat Milk on top. Sprinkle cinnamon or cacao powder on top if desired.

> **PRO TIP:** •
> Don't forget the frozen coffee ice cubes from the Cold Brew recipe (page 355) if serving cold. Coconut Whipped Cream (page 299) is also a delicious addition in place of the Oat Milk.

FROM THE KITCHEN

Cold Brew

MAKES ABOUT 3 CUPS OF COLD BREWED COFFEE
PLUS 12 TO 13 ICE CUBES, APPROXIMATELY 4 SERVINGS
OF COLD BREW DEPENDING ON THE SIZE OF THE GLASS

4   cups medium coarsely ground
    coffee, freshly ground in a coffee
    grinder (burr preferred)

1. In a container that can hold approximately 10 cups, combine the coffee with 6 ½ cups water, stirring vigorously until all the grounds are saturated.

2. Cover and let sit for 24 hours at room temperature, away from sunlight. (For deeper or stronger coffee, brew longer, up to another 24 hours in the fridge.)

3. Strain the coffee through a fine-mesh strainer or nut milk bag. Pour half the liquid into ice cube molds and freeze for at least 6 hours, and chill the other half in the fridge.

4. Serve with the coffee ice cubes from the frozen molds.

Oat Milk

Oat milk has become fairly easily to find and one of the most beloved plant milks. Sustainably grown in most regions, affordable, and foams like a champ, Oat Milk is also easy to learn to make at home. In less than 5 minutes, you can save the boxed waste from your favorite store-bought oat milk and have fresh oat milk just the way you like it, whenever you want.

¾ cup rolled raw oats

1 tablespoon liquid cane sugar

¼ teaspoon vanilla extract

1. Combine all ingredients in a high-speed blender, add 24 ounces cool, filtered water, and blend on high for 1 minute. Make sure all the oats are completely pulverized.

2. Strain through a nut milk bag to remove any solids. (There should be very few solids if the oats have been properly pulverized.)

3. To foam, return the mixture to the blender to create foamy air bubbles. The Oat Milk should be thick and slightly sticky. If making for later, transfer to a liquid storage container with a tight-fitting lid and keep for up to 5 days in the refrigerator.

4. If you have a milk frother, froth the milk until you achieve a nice, robust foam. If you don't, heat the milk on medium and whisk vigorously and constantly until it bubbles and froths. An immersion blender or hand mixer helps achieve these results.

Drinking Chocolate

A step above hot chocolate, this is the death-by-chocolate version of hot cocoa, perfect for the serious chocoholics among your family and friends. Rich and decadent and served spicy, sweet, or bittersweet, this treat deserves slow sipping with your eyes closed.

1 cup high-quality, organic dark chocolate chips (70 to 80 percent dark)

2 cups rice milk or other thin homemade Plant Milk (page 33)

2 cups full-fat coconut milk (canned)

¼ cup maple syrup, or less to taste

1 ½ teaspoons vanilla extract

1 teaspoon cornstarch

¼ teaspoon cinnamon powder, and more for garnishing

¼ teaspoon salt

1 teaspoon crushed red pepper (optional)

1. Melt the chocolate chips in a saucepan over low heat.

2. When the last peaks from the chips are melted, whisk in the rice milk and 1 cup of the coconut milk.

3. Combine the remaining cup of coconut milk, 1 tablespoon of the maple syrup, ½ teaspoon of the vanilla extract, and the cornstarch in a zip-top bag to make the cream. Place the bag in a large food-grade plastic storage container surrounded by ice and let sit, shaking occasionally.

4. To the melted chocolate mixture, add up to 3 more tablespoons maple syrup, to taste, with the cinnamon, salt, crushed red pepper, if using, and the remaining 1 teaspoon vanilla extract in a saucepan. Swirl well to combine thoroughly.

5. Simmer for 2 minutes over medium heat, then divide among small tea cups.

6. Take the zip-top bag with coconut milk and crush slightly to smooth out the thickened mixture. Cut a small corner off the bottom of the bag, and squeeze the cream mixture on top of each drink. Sprinkle with cinnamon and serve.

Apple Cider

MAKES 6 TO 8 SERVINGS

When it is apple season it is also cider season, and with good reason. Cider is the ingenious end result of farmers with too many, or too bruised, apples in a hurry to put them to good use. I like to go apple picking and snack on some, bake with some, and make the rest into cider. Use this classic and simple recipe to convert fresh apples into cider, and feel free to adjust the sugar to your taste preferences.

6 or 7 Gala apples (2 pounds)

½ cup demerara sugar, or more or less to taste

2 whole cinnamon sticks

4 whole cloves

Pinch nutmeg powder

1. Set a sous vide machine to 150°F.

2. Core the apples, reserving the cores. Chop the apples, and remove the seeds and stems from the cores. Discard the seeds and stems.

3. Place the chopped apples, apple cores, and all the remaining ingredients, plus 6 cups filtered water, in a vacuum-sealed or zip-top bag and seal using the water immersion method (page 317). Lower into the sous vide bath, and let sit for 2 hours.

4. After 2 hours, remove the bag from the bath and pour its contents into a heat-safe mixing bowl. Mash the ingredients together with a fork, then return to bag and to the sous vide bath for 1 more hour.

5. Remove the bag from the heat and pour the contents through a sieve to strain. Use a masher to press down on the apple pulp and strain all the liquid out.

6. Serve the cider hot immediately, or use to make Mulled Cider (page 359).

Mulled Cider

Mulled cider is as much about drinking as it is a seasonal potpourri for your home, the perfect mood-setter for family gatherings. I chose my favorite winter fruit, the persimmon (the fuyu is best for sweetness as the other common type, hachiya, can be a bit astringent) to complement the traditional apple. You can also substitute with a winter pear (like bosc or d'anjou) if it's easier to find or your preference.

7	cups Apple Cider (page 358)	2	whole cinnamon sticks
½	cup maple syrup	1	teaspoon fennel seeds
3	palm-sized persimmons, 1 sliced and 2 juiced	1	teaspoon whole allspice
		1	teaspoon vanilla bean powder
5	whole cloves		

1. Set a sous vide machine to 140°F. (Or if making immediately after the Apple Cider, lower the sous vide temperature by 10°F.)

2. Combine all ingredients in a clean vacuum-sealed bag or zip-top bag, seal using the water immersion method (page 317), and place in the sous vide machine to cook for 2 ½ hours.

3. Remove the bag from the heat and pour the contents through a sieve to strain. Serve hot.

Thai Chai Iced Tea

Thai iced tea is one of my favorite sweet treats when I can find it vegan. The hallmark red Thai tea turns orange when combined with sweetened condensed milk, and has a truly unique flavor with vanilla and tea notes. Combining two of my favorite powerful tastes, chai and Thai tea, here you'll get a sweet and creamy, boldly spiced tea you'll want to drink often.

5 cardamom seeds removed from whole pods	Small pinch saffron
½ teaspoon fennel seeds	One 1-inch fresh ginger root, scored
1 teaspoon Garam Masala (page 31)	¼ cup dried Thai tea blend
3 whole cloves	2 tablespoons dried Assam tea leaves
One 2-inch piece of cinnamon bark (not curled cinnamon stick)	2 cups full-fat coconut milk (canned)
Small pinch freshly ground black pepper	1 or 2 tablespoons maple syrup (optional)

1. Grind the whole spices, then combine with the other spices, teas, ginger root, and 2 cups water in a saucepan over medium heat. Stir frequently as the mixture warms, and avoid letting it boil.

2. Remove from the heat and strain through a fine tea strainer. Let cool.

3. In a separate bowl, whisk the coconut milk with the maple syrup, if using.

4. Serve the tea over ice with the sweetened coconut milk.

Golden Mylk

My go-to drink after an intense power yoga class, Golden Mylk is as restorative to sore muscles as it is delicious to drink. Turmeric gives it the signature color and key muscle soothing benefits, while the ginger, vanilla, and cinnamon complement the rich coconut milk and add their own healing benefits. Black peppercorn adds some dimension and heat to the ginger and cinnamon, as well as aids in the absorption of the beneficial curcumin compound within the tumeric.

1 can full-fat coconut milk (approximately 13 ounces)

¼ cup vanilla plant milk, preferably unsweetened, or homemade Plant Milk (page 33) with ¼ teaspoon vanilla extract

3 tablespoons maple syrup, or more or less to taste

1 ½ tablespoons grated fresh ginger

1 ½ teaspoons turmeric powder or 2 ½-inch turmeric root, freshly ground

Scant ½ teaspoon crushed black peppercorns

¼ teaspoon cinnamon powder, and more for garnishing

1 cinnamon stick, broken into 3 pieces

1 whole clove

Pinch Himalayan salt, and more to garnish

1. Combine all ingredients in a saucepan over medium heat. Heat, whisking vigorously, until the color becomes a rich golden brown and steam and light bubbles appear, then strain directly into tea cups for serving.

2. Garnish each serving with a sprinkle of Himalayan salt and cinnamon powder.

Matcha Lemonade

Matcha is my favorite way to start the day, but matcha lemonade is great all day long, especially on hot summer days in the sun. The calendula syrup tastes just like honey, and the sweetness balances out the bitter grassy flavor of matcha. Matcha Lemonade is happiness in a cup, brightly colored, sweet, and bursting with energy and antioxidants.

Calendula Simple Syrup

½ cup whole dried calendula flowers (chamomile can be substituted)	1 ½ cups organic cane sugar

Lemonade

2 ½ tablespoons organic matcha powder (ideally deep green ceremonial grade)	3 cups freshly squeezed Meyer lemon juice (about 11 Meyer lemons)
	Meyer lemon slices for serving

1. Boil 2 cups water in a small saucepan, then reduce to a simmer.

2. Add the calendula flowers and simmer for 7 minutes.

3. Strain to remove the flowers, and return the liquid to the saucepan.

4. Stir in the cane sugar and bring the mixture to a light boil.

5. Maintain a light boil for 15 minutes, stirring constantly, to reduce the liquid.

6. Remove the Calendula Simple Syrup from the heat, and measure out ¼ cup and 1 ¼ cups separately. (Any excess can be reserved for later use.)

7. Combine the ¼ cup warm syrup and the matcha powder in a mixing bowl and whisk to combine.

8. In a separate bowl, combine the remaining 1 ¼ cups syrup, the Meyer lemon juice, and 3 cups water. Divide in half, transfer one half to ice cube trays, and freeze to make lemonade ice cubes.

9. Add the matcha syrup mixture to the remaining half of the lemonade and stir until completely dissolved and mixed. If the matcha doesn't dissolve completely, use a high-speed blender to completely integrate.

10. Chill in the fridge for at least 2 hours, then serve cold over the lemonade ice with the Meyer lemon slices.

ACKNOWLEDGMENTS

Tina would like to thank:

Thanks to the furthest moon and back to my husband, Jon Devoe, for his constant support and encouragement. Also to my foodie child, Harmony Belle, for taste-testing everything in this book and being a cookbook lover and avid eater of plants. Thanks also to my dad, my first foodie example, and to my mom for all the food-love memories. I am so grateful to be part of this book and to share my work and life with others who enjoy the beauty of plant-based food!

Thank you to Jeremy Ogusky (@bostonpotter) for allowing us to use his ceramics, and to Amy Larson (@overseasoned_amy) for allowing us to use her props.

ABOVE: Tina's daughter, Harmony Belle, enjoying the White Chocolate Bergamot Crème Brûlée (page 335)

OPPOSITE, CLOCKWISE FROM TOP LEFT:
Quiche or Frittata (page 163)
Watermelon Gazpacho (page 213)
Sunday Roast (page 227)
Tortilla Taco Bowl (page 123)
Flame-Grilled Stuffed Poblano Peppers (page 254)
Ahi Tuna Steak with Wasabi Coconut Peas (page 257)
Escargot Amuse-Bouche (page 184)

Chef Suzi would like to thank:

My sister, Alex, for being the first vegan in my life, and also my greatest critic. Mom and Dad, Leonard, and Ronna for mostly tolerating my vegan pledge and mostly enjoying my food. Blossom on 9th Avenue for really helping me to see that the future was vegan for this foodie. H-mart—what would I do without you? Isa and Doron and all the female vegan chefs out there who inspired me in the '90s and since then. Alice Waters, because you broke the mold and made it all possible, and also for putting local food and chef-directed gardening in the center of the conversation. Liz, even though you're a vegetarian, you played a role in helping me go vegan the second time around and I'll always love you for that. Laura and Audrey, for your sous chef support and early stage recipe testing. Amanda and Noelle for on-set help. Dr. Brian King, homie for life, for introducing me to Apollo Publishers. Ottolenghi for giving me my first real culinary challenge and waking up mainstream haute cuisine to the joy of plant-forward cooking. Grant Achatz, because sometimes I think you are the most amazing human on the planet. The Pressed, Squeeze, True Bistro, and Knight Moves squads for being my Boston FAM. To Brandon, for keeping me always moving forward and trying harder. To my love, Rich, my fellow traveler and my rock, thank you for your enduring love and support (and for editing even though it drove me bonkers). And last but not least, to my fur baby Kali, nineteen years young—for, among other things, adorably mistaking the Sunday Roast for actual meat.

People confuse me. Food doesn't. . . .
I just know what I see.
And I understand it. It makes perfect sense.

—*Anthony Bourdain*

LEFT: Chef Suzi's cat, Kali, eyeing the Sunday Roast (page 227)

INDEX